HEALTH SECRETS FROM THE ANCIENT WORLD

By

John Heinerman

Cassandra Press
San Rafael, Ca. 94915

Cassandra Press
P.O. Box 868
San Rafael, Ca. 94915

Printed in the United States of America.

First printing 1991

ISBN 0-945946-11-2

Library of Congress Catalogue Card Number 91-73460

Front cover art by Gary Hespenheide. Copyright © 1991 Cassandra Press.

TABLE OF CONTENTS

False misconception of Neanderthals/ Neanderthals had super human strength/ Lessons to learn from Neanderthal diet/ The curse of cooking/ How cooked food can change physical appearances/ The harm done to teeth through processed foods/ The advantages of eating meat cooked rare instead of well-done/ Getting well on a caveman diet/ Prehistoric herbal therapy/ The anti-cancer ellagic acid in fruit.

The origin of the enema in ancient Egypt/ The ups and downs to colonics/ The medical benefits of enemas and colonics/ Mental illness previously treated with colonic therapy/ Heart disease benefited from colonics/ Regular bowel movements important in treating rheumatoid arthritis/ Having an enema in a tranquil setting/ A healthy regard for the liver/ Hormonal influence of the heart upon the liver/ Is the liver rather than the heart where human emotions reside?/ Ways to tonify the liver.

Divining for health reasons/ How to cast lots and interpret correctly for personal health knowledge/ Other forms of health divining: Astrology and familiar spirits/ The births of Abraham and Moses attended by great celestial events/ When prognostication by the stars was religiously legitimate/ Connection between the great storm on Saturn detected by astronomers and Saddam Hussein's invasion of Kuwait.

Manna, the food of life/ Could the children of Israel have subsisted on chlorella for 40 years in the wilderness?/ The health advantages

INTRODUCTION

Ancient civilizations had a lot to offer us in the way of good health rules. Before mankind progressed to city dwelling and pyramid building, people ate better foods, it seems. Ironically, the introduction of agriculture, with its domesticated crops and genetically improved animals, along with the discovery of fire, brought about significant changes not only in the way men and women felt but also in how they looked, as well.

But in time, mankind found out how to treat the wide array of newly acquired maladies. The Egyptians took to the enema, the Babylonians and others turned to herbs, and the Hebrews revolutionized their eating habits with a dietary lists of "do's" and "don'ts."

Besides these several remedial approaches, mankind also focused on the philosophical aspects of good health. The Egyptians, Chinese, Indians, Greeks, Romans, and even some Medieval healers thoroughly investigated the mental, emotional, and spiritual levels to good health.

All of these different approaches are carefully laid out here, and the reader can hope to achieve a more fully developed well-being in every true sense of the word!

Dr. John Heinerman
Salt Lake City, UT 84147
Spring of 1991

CHAPTER ONE

A PALEOLITHIC DIET FROM THE DAYS OF THE
CAVE MAN'S MOST RESPECTED ANCESTORS

To most of us the term Neanderthal conjures up images of some-thing less than human—a grunting, shuffling, beetle-browed lout of a beast who prowled the earth during the Ice Age, wearing ragged furs and occasionally pausing just long enough to whack a woman over the head with his trusty club before dragging her back by her hair to his cold, dreary lair. In popular usage, the word is a stinging insult. Calling an unshaven fellow with a tattoo on his forearm a Neanderthal might earn you a quick trip to any local hospital's emergency care unit.

Neanderthals received such a poor reputation among the general public because they were grievously misjudged by the experts. Until only very recently, nearly all paleethnologists regarded Ne-anderthals as a brutish breed of backward louts that, at best, represented an insignificant side branch of the human family tree.

Why did the experts misjudge Neanderthals? One was a scarcity of fossils in the mid-19th century. No one was prepared for the actual sight of a primitive-looking skeleton in the human closet. And when one did appear in the Neander Valley (*Neanderthal* in the old German dialect) just outside of Dusseldorf, Germany in 1856, it brought on a crippling case of ancestral blindness.

Evolutionary ideas were then coming into vogue and may have helped explain the Neanderthals better. But the old Biblical tradi-tions of creationism still dominated public thinking and permitted no room for their consideration. Thus an entire century would pass before scientists finally recovered from this racial and theological ignorance.

A British geologist visited Germany and brought back a plaster-of-Paris cast of the Neanderthal skull to London, where it was proudly exhibited in the British Museum between the skulls of a gorilla and a Negro—pretty typical for the racial attitudes of those days. But the real blame can be squarely laid on the shoulders of a French expert named Marcellin Boule of the French National Museum of Natural History.

This paleontologist allowed not only his sloppy research, but also his obvious petty hatred towards the mentally handicapped to interfere with nearly every aspect of his physical reconstruction of a Neanderthal skeleton excavated from La Chapelle-aux-Saints. The materials he had to work with were well preserved and nearly everything of importance was available in this skeleton. Yet Boule proceeded to commit an astonishing series of errors, which took until late in this century to correct.

He so misconstructed the bones as to make the Neanderthal appear much like an ape from head to toe. He mistakenly arranged the foot bones so that the big toe diverged from the other toes like an opposable thumb. This quirky feature presumably forced the Neanderthal to walk on the outer part of his feet like an ape. Boule's interpretation of the knee joint was equally incorrect—he announced that the Neanderthal couldn't fully extend his leg, thereby resulting in a bent knee joint.

In every respect, the posture of Boule's reconstruction seemed nonhuman. According to Boule, the spine lacked the curves that permit modern man to stand upright. Atop this misshapen spine the head was placed in a very unbalanced position, thrust so much forward that the poor Neanderthal undoubtedly would have sprained his neck if ever he had attempted to look up into the wild blue yonder overhead. If Boule's Neanderthal man resembled any human being at all, then it had to be Victor Hugo's Quasimodo character in *The Hunchback of Notre Dame*.

By far, though, the most devastating conclusion of the study focused on the presumed intelligence (or apparent lack of it) of the man from La Chapelle-aux-Saints. Boule merely glanced as it were at the long, low skull of this particular Neanderthal and was immediately reminded of those unfortunate victims locked up in several large insane asylums in and around Paris. Citing the interior of the skull as support for his erroneous conclusion, Boule determined to his own satisfaction that there just wasn't enough room left inside for the frontal portions of the brain, which at that time was (incorrectly) believed to be the center of higher intelligence. So in mental capabilities this paleontologist ranked this particular Neanderthal down closer to the apes and considerably further from modern man than he should have done.

While Boule was willing to grant the Neanderthals the honor of the genus Homo, he was very careful to relegate them to a separate, aberrant, almost mutant species of subhuman that, thank goodness, had died out a long time ago. In his otherwise orderly but terribly prejudiced mind, they were shuffling, grunting, drooling, smelly, hunchbacked imbeciles of the worst kind.

And because of his excellent reputation as a scholar and with his formidable diligence, it made his errors in judgment all the more serious. Between 1911 and 1913, he published his findings in three comprehensive tomes. Packed with meticulous details and ringing with the utmost confidence, these monographs made a tremendous impact on the scientific world and the public alike.

Boule's slanted views won almost universal acceptance and even inspired some less flattering views from other scholars. Elliott Smith, for one, a noted anthropologist at University College, London, wrote sometime in the 1920s of those uncouth and repellant Neanderthals whose noses resembled animal snouts.

Anthropology textbooks for decades depicted Neanderthals in the slouched, stoop-shouldered, bent-knee posture that Boule had created for them. Even prestigious institutions like the Field Museum of Natural History in Chicago built several dioramas in which these presumed Ice Age idiots were depicted in various driveling, sniveling, scratching poses of exaggerated retardation. Even popular writers such as H. G. Wells fell into Boule's traps of prejudice. According to Wells in his short story, "The Grisly Folk and Their War with Men," the Neanderthals were fearsome creatures who had a very limited vocabulary consisting mostly of the word "ugh."

Old prejudices die hard, and it wasn't until 1957 that two anatomists took another, more detailed look at the fossil remains from La Chapelle-aux-Saints that had provided the basis for Boule's misinterpretations. Dr. William Straus of Johns Hopkins University and Dr. A. J.E. Cave of St. Bartholomew's Hospital Medical College in London, discovered that this particular Neanderthal had suffered from a severe case of arthritis, which had affected the formation of the vertebrae and the jaw. They also spotted many other inexplicable mistakes in Boule's reconstruction. With everything fully reconsidered, both doctors found Neanderthal man to be quite human indeed.

Thus, by removing the taints of apishness and imbecility that had long been associated with Neanderthals, the Straus-Cave study effectively revived the Neanderthal's candidacy as possible ancestors of modern man. With the overthrow of the corrupted Bouleian vision by the Straus-Cave clarifications, the Neanderthals are placed squarely within the human fold. And we, as their distant relatives, proudly stand on their big, burly shoulders.

As famed Princeton University anthropologist, C. Loring Brace, observed in the February, 1964 issue of *Current Anthropology*: he always objected to the caricature of Neanderthal man that Boule foisted upon the world world. Neanderthal is among the most respected ancestors of contemporary man.

Near East Specimens of Genuine Health

Since the principal theme of our text concerns health secrets from the ancient Near East, it's only reasonable to begin this first chapter with a summary of the archaeological evidence gleaned from two important sites in Shanidar Valley near the dusty village of Zawi Chemi Shanidar in northern Iraq. For here can we see that some of the world's best, brightest, and strongest Neanderthals worked and played in an orderly atmosphere marked by good dietary habits, primitive religious ideas, concern for the helpless, and tender respect for the dearly departed. In other words, what the data are intended to show is that they were no different than most of us in thoughts, emotions, and common health sense. As science writer John Pfeiffer said in the Spring, 1971 *Horizon*, in reference to our Stone Age ancestors, we seem to have a lot in common with them.

According to an anthropologist from Columbia University who was one of the primary excavators at the Shanidar sites, this was where the long preface to Mesopotamian history began. Ralph S. Solecki, in the Jan. 18, 1963 issue of *Science*, noted that when he and his team reached a level known as Shanidar V in their diggings (about 44,000 B.C.), they found evidence denoting violence, compassion, and a regard for the dead.

Continuing the report of their exciting discoveries in Vol. 17 of the journal, *Sumer*, Dr. Solecki mentioned that, in regard to one particular skeleton, it appeared as though the person had been killed by a falling rock. Further analysis of this prehistoric accident shed even greater light on the culture of a Stone Age people who, up until only recently, had been the object of ridicule in much of the scientific world. Solecki's revelations indicate something about the care and concern shown for the less fortunate and handicapped in those times of difficult survival. He said that the accident victim (denoted as Shanidar I) was evidence of prehistoric compassion. In his lifetime he had been physically handicapped with the use of just one arm—hardly enough to feed or protect himself in a savage world. Yet his fellowmen accepted him for what he was and took care of his needs.

In appreciation for their support, he made himself as useful as possible around the hearth. Extraordinary wear on his front teeth suggests that he might have used his jaws for grasping in partial substitution for his missing right arm. Those who survived the rock fall returned later to cover their dead companion's body with loose stones, the equivalent of a modern interment in some respects. Loose mammals bones lying about and on top may have been part of some type of funeral feast in celebration of their friend's greatness. Thus, Neanderthals were capable of displaying much affection for their own.

Besides emotions to indicate the true health of an individual or society, there is also the physical makeup. In order to obtain a clearer understanding of their incredible physique and near Herculean strength, we are indebted to Erik Trinkaus, a Harvard University anthropologist, who wrote several books detailing these very things—*The Shanidar Neanderthals* and *The Mousterian Legacy* (both published in 1983).

The adult bones of the Shanidar Neanderthal showed they had strongly built shoulders, arms, and hands with especially well-developed muscles to grasp and rotate the limbs. Furthermore, their thighs, legs, ankles, and feet indicated a much more robust massiveness to them than more recent humans. More amazing still was that Neanderthal women had larger anterior pelvic dimensions, and hence larger pelvic aperture diameters which allowed them to give birth more easily than is generally the case for humans today. This *significant* difference between the anterior pelvic morphologies of the Shanidar women and modern human females strongly suggests that the Neanderthals may have had gestation periods of up to 12 months. Such gestation periods approximate those expected for mammals, whereas anatomically modern humans have relatively short gestation periods (usually 9 months).

Trinkaus postulates that with their overall muscular development, larger muscles, and thumbs capable of exerting exceptional force during normal grips, Neanderthal men and women were undoubtedly capable of incredible feats of strength that today can usually be performed by only the fewest of muscle-bound body builders. Much of this he attributes to their diet and, in the case of Neanderthal women's longer gestation periods, to many long walks and frequent exercise. Several other anthropologists have even gone so far as to suggest that Shanidar men had the strength to lift the front ends of cars, bend steel with their bare hands, or completely crush a modern guy's hand in an average, everyday handshake.

Lessons to Learn from Neanderthal Diet

In *The Mousterian Legacy*, Trinkaus notes with a touch of evident sadness that the Samson-like physique and strength of these Shanidar residents failed to carry over in later anatomically modern humans. There were more noticeable reductions in potential strength in the power grip, accompanied by a generally weaker hand grip; and a decrease in overall muscularity from

Neanderthal to more modern-looking humans.

A major reason for such expected changes may be directly traced to three major influences in human cultural advancement. The first of these has been explored in a paper by a colleague of mine, H. Leon Abrams, Jr. Dr. Abrams is an associate professor of anthropology at ECJC, University System of Georgia in Swainsboro and had his report on "Fire and Cooking as a Major Influence on Human Cultural Advancement" published in Vol 38 of *Journal of Applied Nutrition*. The technology of utilizing fire, with its expanded application for food preparation, profoundly affected the human race some 40,000 to 50,000 years ago with the advent of Cro-Magnon man.

The second of these was touched upon by a UCLA Medical School professor of physiology, Jared Diamond, in the May, 1987 issue of *Discover* magazine in a short essay appropriately entitled, "The Worst Mistake in the History of the Human Race," Dr. Diamond wrote that early farming practices were very bad for human health.

The first reason for this is that hunter-gatherers like these Shanidar Neanderthals were used to a very diverse diet, whereas early farmers obtained most of their staples from only several starchy crops. The latter gained cheap calories but at the cost of bad nutrition. Interestingly, the same thing is being repeated today, where three high-carbohydrate foods, namely wheat, corn, and rice, make up the bulk of calories consumed by mankind; yet each one is deficient in certain vitamins or amino acids.

Hunting-gathering society didn't farm until circumstances forced them to. And when they finally made the switch it was done so at a cost to their own health. Longevity declined appreciably in post-agricultural communities, where the average lifespan dropped to 19 years from a previous high of around 26.

Secondly, the introduction of agriculture encouraged people to abandon their disease-free nomadic lifestyles and become residents of cities replete with sickness due to overcrowding. Epidemics like tuberculosis, influenza, measles, and plague only came into being when men started living together in confined spaces.

Besides malnutrition, famine, and widespread sickness, agriculture brought on class divisions. In the old hunting-gathering societies, everyone shared the food they got. There was no such thing as long-term food storage and little chance for hoarding. No one person kept all the food to himself and demanded servitude from his fellowmen in exchange for something to eat, as later became common in farming societies.

The advancements made in tool production were a third factor which helped Neanderthals evolve into more civilized humans. M. F. Ashley Montague's book *Culture and the Evolution of Man* touches on this. As Stone Age tools of the Mousterian era became transformed into more sophisticated technology in the Upper Paelolithic culture, there was a subsequent disappearance of the typical Neanderthal facial type. Likewise, there was a reduction in tooth size (the incisor-canine) with greater reliance on tools. When tool refinement reached the point where they became more efficient than teeth for various tasks (chewing leather, grinding seeds), then jaw and tooth sizes shrank.

The lessons learned from Neanderthal diet thus far are: (A) cooking affects the human race; (B) farming of crops yielded more food that was less nutritious; and (C) tool advancement brought a further refinement in food and overall reductions in jaw and tooth sizes. None of these factors prevailed during most of the Neanderthal period. Food was consumed mostly in its raw, unrefined state and thus required considerable mastication before it could be swallowed. And a great deal of chewing meant a lot of exercise for neck and jaw muscles and teeth. Obviously, the more grinding food needed, the thicker and stronger would be the muscles in the faces and necks of hungry Neanderthals.

Secondly, Neanderthals were hunters-gatherers; they foraged in the wild for their daily meals. Such human grazing was quite similar to what Adam and Eve did during their stay in the Garden of Eden.

Rolf L. Wirsing observed in *Current Anthropology* (June 1985) that hunting-gathering cultures seldom ever suffer from mal-and undernutrition, but farming groups do. A diverse diet minimizes the likelihood of nutritional deficiencies. An example used concerned the separate diets of two different Tiruya communities in the Philippines. The first group of men continued their traditional fishing, hunting, and gathering activities, while the second group engaged in farming and sold some of their crops for cash in the marketplace. All the food consumed by one volunteer from each village was weighed and recorded for a year. The hunting-fishing-gathering fellow was discovered to have consumed over a hundred different species of wild and domesticated plants and animals, while the man from the agricultural village ate just forty types of food and relied heavily upon purchased foods.

Also the fellow eating a wide variety of wild game and foods suffered virtually no ill health effects, while the one eating domesticated foods experienced obesity, hypertension, and heartburn. Similar comparisons have been made with Australian aborigines, who, according to the *Journal of Dental Research* (46:812, No. 5 Supplement, 1967), showed some physical similarities to the long extinct Skhul Neanderthaloids of many millenniums ago. Like their Stone Age counterparts from the Mount Carmel area in the

Middle East, these Australian aborigines have the biggest teeth in the world!

If the Australian aborigines compare favorably in certain physical resemblances to these ancient Near Eastern Neanderthals, then would it not stand to reason that their diets could have been similar as well? Carrying this idea further, might not the Neanderthals from Mt. Carmel have become overweight, diabetic, and afflicted with coronary heart disease if they had switched from their own healthy fare to our typical junk food cuisine?

Well, the speculation doesn't need to go very far in order to be reasonably substantiated. Three Australian doctors published an interesting report in the medical journal, *Lipids* (21:684-90, 1986) regarding what happens to aborigines who leave their wilderness foods and adopt purely modern, so-called Western eating habits instead. Within a short time, they become fat, diabetic, and prone to atherosclerosis because of the high sugar and cholesterol contents of the refined foods they're consuming. But when they revert back to the desert again and commence foraging for the natural, unprocessed foods in the wild, most of these diseases soon clear up.

Isn't this then sufficient proof that a *diversity* of foods, preferably as unrefined and unprocessed as possible with only minimal cooking required, is much better to pursue than staying with just a dozen or so basic types of food spawned by modern agriculture. Colin Simpson, in his study of aboriginal Australia entitled, *Adam in Ochre*, noted that one reason why these natives seldom ever get fat is simply because they never ate at any regular time! This speaks well for frequent light snacking of low-fat, low-sodium, and low-sugar foods instead of the customary three square meals a day.

The Curse of Cooking

The reader might have noticed prior to this that hardly any commentary was made upon the negative aspects of cooking. Having been a chef in a restaurant myself for almost seven years and knowing the harmful health effects caused by cooking, I decided to reserve an entire section within this first chapter just for it. In what is to follow, the reader will learn how cooking, *more than anything else* has a dramatic effect upon the shape and size of the face, jaws, and teeth.

Hisashi Suzuki, a professor of anthropology at the University of Tokyo in Japan, dwelled at length on the physical impact which cooked food has had on not only advanced Stone Age cultures, but also more recent Japanese aristocrats as well in *The Amud Man and His Cave Site*. He began by pretty much reiterating the same observations that other anthropologists have made in times past—

that cooked food in prehistoric times tended to gradually free the chewing muscles from their heavy load needed for the lever action of the jaw. This subsequent weakening of the chewing muscles led to the recession of the subnasal part of the upper face, which is tantamount to the reduction of the upper jaw, which is to say that cooked food greatly altered the entire facial appearance of most prehistoric cultures following Neanderthal demise.

Suzuki mentioned that this upper Paleolithic reduction of masticatory organs (due to the discovery of fire) was an added factor in the typical facial changes recognized in Japanese aristocrats over the past two-and-half centuries. Take the Tokugawa Shogunate family, for instance (they reigned from the early 17th century until the mid-19th century). Their origins can be traced to the common people of feudalist Japan. After taking political control of their nation, these family members quickly differentiated themselves from the contemporary common folks in facial characteristics. Of the several changes which became evident in the course of time, none were so remarkable as that which occurred with their chewing apparatus. Such features included: much smaller upper and lower jaws with no indications of wearing of the occlusal surfaces of the teeth even in the elderly; protruding chins; poor growth of the tuberosities for all oral muscles and the trajectorial structure of the lower jaw. He attributed such embarrassing changes to softer and overcooked foods, which required a lot less chewing. Such changes, he insisted, along with family in-breeding, gave them the "ultramodern" look of today's Japanese.

One doesn't even have to go back to the era of Japanese Shoguns, much less another 40,000 years to observe the unfortunate facial characteristics which resulted from eating well-cooked foods. You only need to visit any elementary grade school in the U.S. or Canada and study the children's faces, as I have repeatedly done, to witness the same miserable outcome. The extremely receded, often pinched look of the subnasal portion of the upper face, the smaller, rounded, weaker-looking jaw, the unevenly spaced, often crooked teeth requiring braces, and an overall poorly constructed appearance usually denote early childhood diets consisting primarily of overly cooked foods that needed very little, if any, chewing. Also, such children are often more prone to ear, nose, and throat infections and are more apt to be mouth-breathers, than kids who have been raised on raw or semi-cooked foods that obviously demanded a great deal of chewing. Such kids are easy to spot, simply because they're so rare to find— they're the ones with the well-angled noses, larger subnasal apertures, squarer jaws, firmer chins, evenly spaced and nicely arranged teeth and more completed or finished looks to their facial features. As a rule, such individuals breathe through their nasal passageways, as it was intended to be, instead of through their mouths as so many other young children do.

Undoubtedly, most parents probably aren't even aware of the heavy toll that mushy or soft, processed foods exact from their preschool youngsters in terms of undeveloped or half-finished facial characteristics. A food list longer than both of my arms together is to blame for this. Gerber baby foods, Wonder Bread, Twinkies, sugary cereals, McDonald's hamburgers, most canned fruits and vegetables, soda pop and cola drinks, not to mention mom's own overly cooked meals.

Irrefutable evidence that cooked and processed foods cause extreme dental and facial development problems in the growing youth comes from none other than a doctor of dental surgery, Weston A Price, D.O.S. He travelled the world during the mid-1930s and studied tens of thousands of primitive peoples, comparing those who subsisted mostly on raw, natural foods with those who had switched to the refined, overly cooked foods of modern man. His resulting book, *Nutrition and Physical Degeneration* (Redlands, Calif. 1939) remains a rare, out-of-print classic even 52 years later! Renowned Harvard anthropologist, Earnest A. Hooton wrote the distinguished foreword to it, noting that this dentist possessed the scientific horse sense to supplement his knowledge of the probable causes of dental disease with a study of the dietary regimens associated with dental health. Hooton observes that if savages know enough to eat the things which keep their teeth healthy, they are more intelligent in dietary matters than we are. This is why he described Dr. Price's invaluable work as being an important book.

Price took thousands of photographs of children or young adults who either subsisted entirely on a nearly uncooked diet or else depended wholly on processed, cooked foods. It is these photographic comparisons which make the book so important, from an anthropological perspective.

His exhausting ordeal through much of heated Africa revealed further damage done to tooth, jaw, and facial development in those brought up on well-cooked, highly processed foods. He covered about 6,000 miles in Africa and came into contact with about 30 different tribes. Special attention was given to the foods, samples of which were obtained for chemical analysis. Over 2,500 negatives were made and developed in the field. There was a sharp contrast between the health and ruggedness of the primitives in general and that of the foreigners who have entered their country. Their superior ruggedness was not racial because when they came into contact with modern civilizations, degenerative processes developed.

A marked variation of the incidence of illnesses was found in the different tribes. This variation could be directly associated with the nutrition rather than with the tribal pattern. The lowest percentage of irregularity occurred in the tribes living mostly on dairy products and marine life.

While the primitive racial stocks of Africa developed normal facial and dental arch forms when on their native foods, several characteristic types of deformity often developed in the children of the modernized groups. One of the simplest forms, that also corresponds with a very common deformity pattern in the United States, involves the dropping inward of the laterals with narrowing of the upper arch making the incisors appear abnormally prominent and crowding the cuspids outside the line of the arch.

Having worked in the restaurant business myself for almost seven years during my high school and early college years, I was especially intrigued by one example in particular that he used to show the marked differences between mostly uncooked versus cooked, processed foods. He examined the native servants of a tourist hotel on Lake Kivu. An examination of 320 teeth of ten individuals revealed 20 teeth with caries. All of these carious teeth were in the mouth of one individual, the cook! The others all boarded themselves and lived on native foods, while the cook used European foods.

Wherever Price went throughout the world he found the same recurring themes over and over again. Diets with very little cooked or processed foods produced healthy facial and dental arch development, but where processed and highly cooked foods prevailed, there would invariably be many facial and dental arch deformities and numerous skeletal defects.

Occasionally Dr. Price was able to compare natives subsisting on traditional diets with white children fed primarily cooked, processed foods. Where such comparisons were possible, the results were quite striking. Among the Torres Strait Islanders, he photographed school children from two groups cn Thursday Island. Commenting on the evident differences between the two groups, he noted the beautifully proportioned faces of the natives, and the pinched nostrils and marked disturbance in proportions of the faces of the whites. The dental arches of the natives are broad, while many of the whites have very crowded teeth. The parents and children of the natives used native foods while the parents and children of the whites used modern imported foods.

During my latter mid-teenage years, I worked one entire summer in a cannery in Provo, Utah, where some of my young adulthood was spent. I can recall all the fresh vegetables which came into the plant by truck. These were unloaded from big, heavy wooden containers and dumped into a giant hopper to be transferred onto a conveyer belt inside the plant where they were washed, cleaned, and sorted before being boiled in huge kettles until they were nearly soft in texture. Working on the loading dock as I did then, I remember just how sweet and delicious and crunchy those peas, snap beans, and carrots were when consumed in their raw rather than cooked-to-death form. That is probably why I have never been a big fan of canned vegetables. That particular summer was probably one of the healthiest moments in my life, from a Neanderthal foraging perspective. Since I seldom packed a lunch of white bread and peanut-butter-and-jelly or white bread and bologna sandwiches as the other kids my age did, I usually resorted to my own hunting-and-gathering from the various bins of raw vegetables waiting to be processed. Thus it is very easy for me to appreciate Price's observations regarding the ill health and poor facial development of the white school teacher's boy.

The harmful health effects experienced from cooked foods have also been pointed out by some medical doctors. Among them are Henry G. Bieler, M.D. For over 50 years as a general practitioner, Dr. Bieler treated thousands of people from all walks of life: Hollywood movie stars like Greta Garbo and Gloria Swanson, syndicated newspaper columnists such as Hedda Hopper, wealthy Pasadena dowagers, California politicians, Missouri farmers, Kentucky coal miners, and Ohio school children, to name just a few.

His innovative approach, certainly for those days at least, was mainly to treat health problems by prescribing healing foods instead of synthetic drugs. In almost all cases using drugs to treat patients is harmful, he noted in his best-seller, *Food Is Your Best Medicine.* Dr. Bieler was one of only a very few medical doctors who believed that the majority of diseases was induced by overcooked and processed foods, resulting in an impairment and breakdown of body cells, thereby opening the way for viral infections.

Overcooking animal protein, he maintained, produces more toxic wastes in the urine, in sweat, and in other body secretions. An understanding of colloidal chemistry helps here: raw protein is hydrophile colloid, while the cooked form is hydrophobe colloid. The latter is harder to digest because of the manner in which the molecules have been arranged. An example of this may be seen in a raw egg white vs. that of a hard-boiled one.

The first is easily digested with no intestinal putrefaction to speak of, while the latter takes longer to be broken down and can result in some flatulence, signifying minor putrefaction.

If meat is to be cooked at all, he suggested that it be done rare or medium rare, never medium or well-done. Also, I might add, meat should never be charbroiled, grilled, fried or microwaved, and should not be eaten with deep-fried foods. Steamed zucchini squash is one of the best vegetables to help tonify an overtaxed liver.

Bieler then cited the work of the now deceased Francis F. Pottenger, Jr., to further demonstrate the bad effects of cooked protein on other biological systems, particularly cats.

As long as Pottenger fed his cats raw protein and nothing else they remained virtually disease-free. In his lengthy five-year study, he used 109 cats. Kittens born of mothers subsisting on raw protein alone, were healthy also and lived out their entire lives in pretty good health.

However, when cats were introduced to cooked meat similar to what humans prefer, they became afflicted with many different maladies: disease, tooth and hair loss, brittle bones, arthritis, heartburn, liver problems, brain, spinal cord, and degenerations. He summed up his findings in several ways: (1) cats thrived on raw protein, while others took sick and experienced premature deaths on cooked meat; (2) cats injured by heated protein diets could never completely regain their health, even though switched back to raw protein again; (3) liver impairment in felines given cooked protein was gradual and their resulting excrements actually proved harmful as fertilizer for garden plants; (4) the first generation of kittens from such felines were abnormal, the second were usually still-born or diseased at birth. There was no third litter as such felines had by then become totally sterile—all as a result of eating cooked meat and heated milk.

Interestingly, the cooked proteins used in the Pottenger cat experiments consisted of boiled, irradiated, and pasteurized milk, buttermilk, canned and dried milk, cheese and ice cream, cooked eggs (boiled, fried, and scrambled), cooked meat (boiled, roasted, and charbroiled), and "cured" meats (salted or heat-dried like salt pork or smoked bacon and ham).

Bieler also mentioned that the common belch or digestive *faux pas* which we all suffer from occasionally, is actually nature's way of warning us that something is wrong inside of us. It's another way of the body telling us that cooked and processed foods aren't too good for human health. He insisted that we should pay more heed to this inner voice of the solar plexus.

The bottom line is this: cooked foods digest poorly and create gas and hyperacidity. Cooking also destroys valuable nutrients like enzymes and vitamins. Meats cooked rare to medium-rare, lightly cooked eggs, and raw unpasteurized milk are much easier to digest. Vegetable proteins in the form of nuts, avocados, and legumes are not only healthier but easier for the body to assimilate. Of the starches, boiled or baked potato and cereal grains with their accompanying roughages are important, too.

The work of Drs. Price, Bieler and Pottenger reflect a major consideration as to why the Neanderthal race of prehistoric times enjoyed such remarkably good health.

And why they were similarly endowed with magnificent physiques and amazing strength far beyond the capacities of even our most modern muscle-bound body builders. They ate little or no cooked food to speak of!

Getting Well on a Caveman Diet

This is probably going to come as a shock to some readers who have been led to believe that a vegetarian-oriented diet is healthier for you. If such produce is organically grown, then this concept has obvious merit. But since most of our fruits and vegetables these days are laced with harmful chemical pesticides, it may be wiser in the long run to derive more of your nourishment from undercooked meat, preferably fish, lamb, goat, or beef.

Granted that cattle have their share of growth hormones and antibiotics injected into them directly, or indirectly through their feed. But despite such obvious drawbacks, these kinds of meat should provide a person with most of the essential nutrients that grocery produce would.

In the book, *The Emergence of Man* (part of the Time-Life series), author George Constable imagined what a typical dinner would have been like in prehistoric times. He pictured Neanderthals of both sexes returning to their caves joyfully carrying armloads of freshly killed meat. The liver and fat would have been prized above anything else, followed by the brain, kidney, heart, and lungs. Bones would soon be cracked open to get at the marrow inside, while the soft head of the leg joints would be leisurely chewed on. Even the undigested vegetative contents of a reindeer's pair of stomachs would be consumed.

Above all, though, Neanderthals loved their bone marrow! I recall an episode from my early youth in Provo, Utah. My father, who owned and operated Cottage Book Shop, would do our daily shopping at Speckart's Market just a block away. He would often get a nice soup bone and make a delicious vegetable beef soup with it. My brother, Joseph, and I used to clamor for the marrow from the cooked bones and enjoy spreading it on some wheat or rye toast, then lightly salting it before eating. This "poor man's caviar" as we used to call it, gave us plenty of the necessary trace elements we needed. The quality of the meat to be consumed was important to the Neanderthals. Mammoths, caribou, and elk fed on numerous grasses and sedges, which were all rich in mineral salts, beta carotene and vitamin C, according to *Quarternary Research* (23: 123-29, 1985). Secondly, the meat was lean, but still had plenty of cholesterol, observed *The Wall Street Journal* in an article on cave man diet, published October 21st, 1986. Despite this, however, it suggests that fat, *not* cholesterol poses the dietary problems, the *Journal* concluded.

Two short articles on this same theme were published simultaneously in the May, 1985 issue of *American Health* magazine. The one article, reporting on prehistoric diet, noted that Stone Age meat had much less fat on it than today's meat does. Modern cattle carcasses are often 30% fat vs. 3.9% in free-living African and North American game. Early meat moreover had fewer calories and more protein per unit of weight.

The second report concerned a highly interesting if not somewhat controversial study completed by Dr. Vivian Bruce of the University of Manitoba. In her research, she discovered that there was no difference in the total cholesterol levels between people fed diets of beef-based proteins and those fed vegetable proteins. She concluded that there really wasn't much point to eliminating meat entirely from the diet.

Dr. Bruce had eight healthy young male volunteers form two groups. One group ate all their protein from vegetable sources for 21 days, the other ate a diet of 55% beef protein and 45% vegetable protein. Then they switched. Both diets contained equal amounts of fat and wheat fiber. The beef not only did not raise LDL (bad) cholesterol levels; it actually elevated levels of HDL (good) cholesterol) The all-important HDL/LDL ratio rose during the beef diet. This happened despite the fact that the beef-protein diet actually contained two to three times *more* cholesterol than the vegetable-protein diet did. So long as fat intake is low, Dr. Bruce insists, eating lean meat won't hurt you. And it can certainly supply the body with a lot of iron, zinc, and copper—elements sometimes difficult to obtain enough of in fruits or vegetables. Eating meat has its good points, she thinks.

Scientists who've lived among modern Neanderthal counterparts, report that despite high meat intake, the fat content in their diet remains very low. Such is what Melvin Konner, M.D., a physician-anthropologist at Emory University in Atlanta, noted during the two years he and his wife spent with the Kung San bushmen of Botswana. He wrote an article about what they learned for the *New York Times Magazine* (June 5, 1988). In which he observed that they get 25% of their dietary fat from wild game. But these wild animals make our leanest cuts of meat from the supermarket seem succulent, even to the point of almost dripping with grease. The Kung do not consume dairy products, following a pattern similar to the Neanderthals in this respect. There is also no bottled oil or canned lard ever used in their cooking. The little bit of fat obtained from wild game is far less saturated and, therefore, less harmful.

A few simple statistical comparisons provided by Konner show how far from prehistoric diets we have wandered. Neanderthals and their modern counterparts averaged only 4.3% fat intake, compared to 25-35% in supermarket meat today. Neanderthal and modern primitives have sodium consumption estimated at 690 mg. daily, as compared to between 2,000-7,000 mg. for present-day Americans. His conclusion is that we are in an unprecedented evolutionary situation, surrounded by constant supplies of fat, sugar, and salt undiluted by fiber.

Stone Age diets were just the opposite of this, as reported in the significant article entitled, "Paleolithic Nutrition," which appeared in the January 31st, 1985, *New England Journal of Medicine*. The foods we now eat are usually divided into four basic groups; meat and fish, vegetables and fruit, milk and milk products, and breads and cereals. But adults living before the development of agriculture derived most of their nutrients from the first two food groups. This was probably broken down into 35% meat and 65% vegetable foods, with cereal grains rarely being consumed. Dairy food was almost never consumed. Hence, the key to rediscovering good Neanderthal health would seem to be in formulating for yourself a diet that is *low* in fat (but *not* necessarily cholesterol), *low* in sugar, *low* in salt, and *high* in vegetable-fruit fibers and *very lean* animal protein.

Duplicating such prehistoric diet, and the exercise which went with it in the hunting and gathering activities, may yield more energy, better health, and an increased chance of beating modern diseases of civilization, such as osteoporosis, obesity, cancer, and heart disease, *The Wall Street Journal* commented in its October 21st, 1986 article.

Prehistoric Herbal Therapy

We conclude our lengthy, introductory chapter on Neanderthal health with some observations about their use of herbs for treating different maladies. The remarkable excavations of those amazing Neanderthal burials were made in 1960 at the Shanidar Cave in the rugged Zagaros Mountains of northern Iraq. Ralph Solecki of Columbia University, as a matter of routine procedure, collected samples of the soil in and around the grave site and sent them to a laboratory at the Musee de l'Homme in France. There his colleague Arlette Leroi-Gourhan checked the pollen content, hoping it would provide useful information on the climate and vegetation prevailing during Neanderthal times. What she discovered, however, was utterly unexpected.

Pollen was present in the grave in unprecedented abundance. Even more astonishing, some of it appeared in clusters and a few clusters had been preserved along with the parts of the flowers that had supported them. No birds or animals or wind could possibly have deposited such material there. Clearly, masses of flowers had been placed in the grave by the companions of the deceased ones.

Microscopic examination of the pollen indicated that it came from numerous species of bright-colored flowers, related to the grape hyacinth, bachelor's button, hollyhock, and grounsel. What is especially intriguing is that many of these same plants are currently used by contemporary peoples in Iraq as poultices and herbal remedies. Solecki, Leroi-Gourhan, and others believe that early Neanderthals employed these plants for their same medicinal properties as well.

This penchant for plants by man may be traced back to his very earliest beginnings. Whether one wishes to go with the anthropological view of primate-to-man evolution or with the Biblical doctrine of a primitive race of men *before* Adam and Eve (see Genesis 1 and 2 for the mention of *two separate* races of humans) is entirely optional. But for our purposes here, we can say that during his various stages of evolution, man has apparently inherited from simian society a *basic genetic trait* for plant preference.

The April, 1981 issue of *Current Anthropology* discussed this in some detail. Anthropologists have observed an overlapping between plant and medicinal foods used by the hunting-gathering bushmen living in the miombo woodlands of eastern and south-central Africa *and* chimpanzees and baboons residing in the same regions. Of nearly 500 plant genera studied by scientists in the wild, which humans and primates rely upon for food and medicine, overall, fruits and, secondarily, leaves and shoots are the most frequent types of staples for humans and chimpanzees, the journal reported.

Such heavy reliance upon fruits, however, isn't without some very positive health consequences. *Science News* for February 9th, 1985 commented that Neanderthal men broke an important rule of modern nutrition by consuming foods from only two food groups—meats and fruits and vegetables. Three years later, this same science periodical reported in its December 3rd, 1988 issue that new studies now suggest that fruits and vegetables—not grains—offer the most beneficial fiber to prevent colon cancer.

What principal ingredient in fruits might be responsible for this unique preventive action? Something called ellagic acid, says

Science News for April 2nd, 1988 and *Cancer Research* for May, 1986. Scientists from the Medical College of Ohio in Toledo state that fruits and nuts may be a gracious hospitality gift and a tasty cancer preventive. Ellagic acid reduced DNA damage caused by harmful chemical compounds occurring in tobacco smoke and auto exhaust, synthetic preservatives in processed meats, and certain dangerous molds formed in spoiled foods. In other words, researchers say, ellagic acid competes for the same DNA receptor sites that are also used by the carcinogens.

Fruits, especially berries, and nuts are high in ellagic acid. Grapes, strawberries, black currants, raspberries, cranberries, black walnuts, Brazil nuts, and cashews, to mention just a few, are extremely high in this important compound. Also, *the hull* or *shells* of some nuts, such as with cashews and black walnuts, are likewise rich in ellagic acid, as reported in the October, 1968 *Journal of Pharmaceutical Sciences.*

Besides taking the above items into the diet in their fresh, raw forms, many of the same can also be found in valuable herbal supplements. For instance, Michael Schwartz, M.D., of San Antonio, Texas, includes several important berries in his Immu-Boost—a product especially designed to increase the power of the immune system to better resist bodily invasion by infectious viruses. Or herbal formula Q_{19} from Quest Vitamins of Vancouver, B.C., which is an excellent rejuvenating tonic consisting of berries, flowers, leaves, shoots, and roots. In either of these products can one find a certain amount of the concentrated plant foods preferred by primates and evolving human beings long ago and their modern counterparts.

We have already mentioned that, at the very least, a primitive understanding of herbal therapy existed in some form before and during man's presumed evolution into the Homo sapien species. But can creatures of lesser intelligence differentiate between good and bad plants. Were the apes that scientists claim men descended from —which is plain nonsense if squared with Biblical history—able to distinguish between beneficial and harmful herbs? Field observations by one scientist in the Costa Rican jungles suggest that primates living several million years ago already had within them an inherent ability to do so and eventually passed this genetic trait along to their descendants.

Kenneth E. Glander wrote about the howler monkeys of Central America in the March 1977 issue of *Natural History* magazine. Their food selection process is nothing short of amazing, he thought. Howlers like to munch on leaves of the madera negra tree; there are some 150 of them within their home range. But the mature leaves are poisonous to rodents, dogs, and horses. However, the monkeys consume them, but not indiscriminately. The group he studied ate the mature leaves of just three of those 150 trees. Members of another primate tribe, which sometimes visited this area of study, also fed on the same three trees.

Two of these trees grew almost side-by-side, while the third one was close to a thousand feet away, on an opposite bank of the Rio Corobici river. And though the howlers swung through many of the other 147 trees throughout their immediate habitat, they never fed on the mature leaves of any of them, even when passing through them on their way to the three good trees. This suggests that there was something very different about this trio of trees, which the monkeys were able to discern. Glander's analyses of leaves from these three madera negras indicated that they lacked certain toxic alkaloids, which leaves from the other 147 trees contained in large amounts.

Thus, these howlers exhibited a natural defense mechanisms by choosing only those parts of the tree with the lowest level of toxins in them. These were the ripe fruits, flowers, and new leaves. The monkeys seldom ate the mature leaves of most other tree species; and, if they did, consumed only limited quantities of them. Instead, they seemed to prefer the leaf stalks best of all. By doing so, they demonstrated their ability to choose plant parts with the least harmful alkaloids in them.

The selective feeding engaged in on particular parts of certain tree species, explains why the monkeys dropped many unchewed leaves to the ground. Originally, scientists imagined this to be a rather wasteful feeding habit, but Glander's research proved it to be the careful selection of safe forage material.

Anthropologists would use this incident to explain how evolved man inherited his own food-selection instincts. But in reality, they were talents endowed to the first man and woman at the time of their creation. Shouldn't we, who are technologically superior, utilize them just as much as our Stone Age ancestors did?

CHAPTER TWO

HOW THEY CLEANSED THE
INNER MAN IN EGYPT AND MESOPOTAMIA

The Origin of The Enema

Probably no bit of history could be as interesting and unusual in scope for health-minded folks as the origin of the enema. It began in Egypt many, many centuries ago and in time took on near cult-like status throughout the land. In fact, as the evidence will show, the anus was undoubtedly second in position only behind the pharoah himself, to be revered and held in such high and noble esteem.

According to ancient Egyptian legend, the god Thoth became distressed over the many diseases among the ancient people living along the banks of the Nile River. Realizing that most of these ailments were due in part or wholly to obstructed bowels, he sent an incarnation of himself in the form of the ibis to show them what to do for constipation.

This crane-like bird has a white body and black head and may be seen even today in great numbers, standing along the banks of the Nile. Now the ibis has a peculiar habit of bending its neck underneath and inserting its long beak into its rectum, as if to flush its insides out. Ancient Egyptians witnessing this came up with the idea to do the same thing with their colons as well. Thus, we find in the Ebers Papyrus one of the earliest references to an enema device —"a cattle horn, its sharp end clipped off so as to create a small opening (for water to run through)."

So popular were enemas that many of the pharoahs had specially appointed physicians who did nothing else but administer enemas to their royal highnesses when occasions required them to. In fact, one such physician had his official court title engraved on the wall of his particular tomb in hieroglyphics: "Guardian of the Royal Bowel Movement." This peculiar piece of history was mentioned in passing by Jurgen Thorwald in his *Science and Secrets of Early Medicine*. Undoubtedly, this ancient individual kept things moving through the Pharoah, as his royal highness kept the affairs of state moving.

Enemas have been around for a long time in other cultures besides the Egyptian. The ancient Maya, for instance, utilized them for achieving greater spiritual enlightenment via the introduction of certain mind-expanding agents into the body through the rectum.

Archaeologists Peter T. Furst and Michael D. Coe discussed such "Ritual Enemas" in the March 1977 issue of *Natural History*. They discovered the ritual use of such intoxicating enemas on artifacts dating from the first millennium A.D. The first evidence of such a thing came to light in 1976 when they carefully examined a painted vase located in a private collection in New York City. The polychrome jar dating from 300-700 A.D. showed a man inserting a syringe into his rectum. The depicted task was carried out by a second man, who also had a another bulbed enema syringe tucked into his belt.

The rectal administration of such intoxicants had definite advantages over the oral route. First, there would be considerably less nausea; and secondly, they would be faster-acting when taken through the rectum than ingested through the mouth into the gut. Once the absorbed liquids hit the bloodstream from the rectum, they're promptly dispatched to the brain for the desired hallucinogenic effects.

Mind-stupefying enemas like this still are somewhat common in a few parts of Middle America. An ethnographer by the name of Tim Knab was doing some linguistic research on his own among the Huichols of western Mexico in the early 1970s. He met an elderly female shaman in the community of Santa Catarina, who still employed an enema device for dispatching peyote in a quick and exhilarating way into her various clients. The bulb portion was made from the bladder of a wild deer and the tube part from the hollow femur of the same animal. She prepared her peyote by grinding it to a fine pulp and diluting with it with sufficient water.

But instead of just taking this mixture by mouth as is common for the Huichols to do, she administered it rectally in the form of a drug enema. This way, her clients, could avoid the bitter, acrid taste and the nausea generally accompanying the oral intake of this hallucinogenic cactus.

The Ups and Downs to Colonics

Besides an enema, there is also a colonic irrigation, which is nothing more than a sophisticated enema using special equipment that creates strong water pressure, exceeding that which can be done with a home enema bag. An enema is usually of short duration (no more than a few minutes at the most), while a colonic irrigation is of much longer duration, up to an hour or more.

But to effectively cleanse the system, other techniques must also be employed, since the water only reaches the lower intestines. A strong adherence to a vegetable, fruit, and juice diet is advised for maximum benefit from the colonics. Other programs could include a series of herbal and vitamin-mineral supplements.

Leo Albi, who owns Albi Imports of Burnaby, B.C., Canada, distributes two of the most popular colon-cleansing products to ever come out of the Orient these days. They are part of his Li Chung Yun herb line, which has proven to be a big hit all over Southeast Asia. The Herbal Laxative 1 contains fine herbs like senna, cascara, sagrada, buckthorn, and rhubarb to help evacuate even the most stubborn and difficult episodes of constipation.

And his L.B.C. (Lower Bowel Capsules) Formula 2 has proven to be a special favorite in some Vancouver, Seattle, San Francisco, and Los Angeles Chinese herb shops, because of the nice tonifying effects it seems to have upon the lower bowels. Either of these fine products can be used in conjunction with or separate from a colonic irrigation. (See the Appendix for additional details on obtaining these products, under Albi Imports).

Caution should always be used, however, when submitting to colonic irrigations administered by any clinic or health professional outside the comfort and convenience of your own home or apartment. The August 5, 1982 *New England Journal of Medicine* contained information about the potentially harmful effects from such therapy.

Between June 1978 and December 1980, about three dozen cases of amebiasis surfaced throughout western Colorado. Every case had eventually been traced to a particular chiropractic clinic which was giving frequent colonic irrigations upon request. Of the 36 infectious cases, ten patients required immediate colectomy, with six of them dying soon thereafter. Of 176 clients who had been to this facility during the September-December 1980 period, about 80 of them had received colonic irrigations and another 96 had received other forms of treatment. Twenty-one percent of this therapy group had bloody diarrhea as a result of treatment, as compared with 1% of the nonirrigation group receiving other care, like spinal manipulation, for example. Thirty-seven percent of the colonic irrigation patients who gladly volunteered stool specimens to the Colorado State Health Department had evidence of amebic infection, as compared with 2.4% in the non-irrigation group.

Patients who were given colonics following someone else with bloody diarrhea, run the greatest risk for developing amebiasis. Routine testing of the colonic irrigation device after general cleaning, showed excessive contamination with fecal coliform bacteria. Public health officials believed that the severe outbreak of this nasty disease was proportionate to the number of individuals getting colonics.

Lack of adequate equipment and tube sterilization with boiling water or hot steam and very short periods between individual colonic treatments, were the factors most cited for such an outbreak.

In all fairness to colon irrigation therapists, it ought to be mentioned here that this Colorado episode is a fairly isolated incidence. Most colon therapists, in fact, are quite hygienic and go to great lengths to assure their clients of a *safe* cleansing experience. Also, this article did point out similar infections have occurred with *hospital*-administered enemas, citing *JAMA* 110:1664 (1938) and 174:1207-8 (1960) as proof of this. Therefore, when utilizing the professional services of a colon therapist, just be sure that his or her facilities operate under principles of *strict cleanliness!*

Medical Benefits of Enemas and Colonics

The occasional benefits to be experienced from enemas and colonics have been highlighted from time to time in the medical literature. The following articles calls some of these to the reader's attention.

E.S. Barghoorn. "Colonic therapy. Its relation to medical practice." *American Journal of Physical Therapy* 8:304-06 (1932). About three-fourths of civilized people are afflicted with some form of intestinal stasis and many other illnesses result. The author gave over 4,000 high colonic irrigations in Dayton (Ohio) in the last 3 years in conjunction with other physical therapy measures to cases referred to him by physicians. Many cases have had some very remarkable results and I believe all have been benefitted.

W. A. Bastedo. "Colonic irrigations." *New England Journal of Medicine* 199:865-66 (1928). It is stated that other uses for colon irrigations are: (1) To clean out the bowel in acute food poisoning, acute dysentery, or acute septic conditions of the bowel; (2) With hot liquids to allay pain in biliary, renal, and mucous colic, pain in the urinary bladder or ureter, and in tuberculous peritonitis; (3) With cold liquids in febrile states.

J. Friedenwald and S. Morrison. "Value, indications, limitations and technique of colonic irrigation." *Medical Clinics of North America* 18:1611-28 (May, 1935). The opinion is expressed that if colonic irrigations are correctly used in selected cases they fulfill an important therapeutic need. The conditions in which they are probably most helpful are mucous colitis and intestinal stasis but there are a number of other dysfunctions in which their occasional use is indicated. The simpler the irrigating fluid the better and it is generally conceded that plain water, salt solution and bicarbonate of soda, properly diluted, are most desirable except in those instances in which some specific medicinal agent is indicated.

J.S. Hibben. "Irrigation of the colon." *Archives of Physical Therapy* 21:33-40 (1940). The local bowel conditions for which colonic irrigation has been advocated include constipation, fecal impaction, amebiasis, diverticulitis, and mucous colitis. The procedure has been recommended for such systemic conditions as rheumatoid arthritis, certain mental diseases, and the symptom—complex chronic intestinal toxemia. Contraindications are severe cardiac diseases, aneurysm, advanced arteriosclerosis, severe anemias, high fevers, gastrointestinal hemorrhage, ulceration or perforation, and hemorrhoids.

F. S. Jameson. "Colonic therapy. Its usefulness for the relief of constipation and systemic diseases and the indications for its employment." *American Medicine* 36:469-474 (1930). To relieve chronic constipation, colonic irrigation is the most successful form of treatment known. Many functional nervous diseases, especially neurasthenia, chronic deforming diseases of the joints, blood dyscrasias (diseased blood), and certain forms of chronic nephritis are benefitted by colonic therapy. In the control of high blood pressure, systematic colon treatments in association with dietary restriction are the most effective forms of treatment yet employed. Symptoms referable to the upper alimentary tract, being often of reflex origin, are in many cases amenable to treatment by colonic irrigation.

N. W. Kaiser. "Colonic therapy in mental disease." *Ohio State Medical Journal* 26:510-16 (1930). During the past year some 70 patients were examined. These were composed of dementia praecox, manic depressive and psychoneurotic types. The treatment of these patients has been limited very largely to colonic irrigations 2-3 times a week. The result of these treatment were often gratifying.

H.K. Marshall and C.E. Thompson. "Colon irrigation in the treatment of mental disease." *New England Journal of Medicine* 207: 454—57 (1932). Colon irrigation produces a quicker return to mental stability in many cases. In active cases sedation is unquestionably obtained, strikingly shown by a reduction in the number of wet sheet envelopments required. Since the use of colon irrigation, wet sheet envelopments have fallen to less than 60 monthly and sometimes none at all. The destruction of mattresses, sheets and clothing has fallen off approximately 50%.

C. L. Rowell. "Colonic therapy." *Archives of Physical Therapy* 10:354—60 (1929). The author considers colonic therapy a cure for pneumonia, influenza, typhoid fever, and acute heart disease. Unless there is some special contraindication these conditions are indications for a cathartic or an enema. By removing the handicap of intestinal toxemia, the patient's natural resistance is given a better chance to overcome the condition from which he is suffering. Consistently good results can be expected in so-called essential hypertension, infective arthritis, skin diseases, and in many chronic condition. There are also various vague symptoms, such as headache, backache, nervousness, anorexia, and insomnia which often respond well to colonic therapy.

R. G. Snyder, et al. "Colonic stasis in chronic arthritis." *Archives of Physical Therapy* 14:610-17;628 (1933). Colonic and terminal ileal stasis and low grade infective processes in the colon and terminal ileum are usually overlooked in treating chronic arthritis. A history of regular bowel movements in arthritic patients does not rule out constipation. Examination of the colon carried out shortly after evacuation will often disclose large masses of fecal material throughout the entire length of the colon in patients who do not complain of constipation.

J. W. Wiltsie. "Colon irrigations and colonic therapy." *American Medicine* 41:213-17;225 (1935). Colonic therapy is indicated with fecal or intestinal stasis, chronic intestinal toxemia, and chronic fecal infection. Possible symptomatic diagnoses and syndromes include high or low blood pressure, arthritis, colitis, gall bladder disease, proctitis (rectal inflammation), pyelitis (renal pelvic inflammation), sinus infection, bilious attacks, indigestion, chronic appendicitis, anemia, certain types of asthma and cardiac disease, headaches, iritis (iris inflammation), certain skin diseases, dizziness, mental and physical depression, neurasthenia (nervous exhaustion), constipation, diarrhea, and others. These conditions are not always the result of intestinal pathology, but usually malfunction of the colon will be found to be a consideration.

A Bottom View on Enemas by the Ancient Egyptians

Some of the foregoing medical articles on the value of enemas and colonic irrigations, emphasize that a myriad of diseases are invariably linked to the colon in some way. The ancient Egyptians held the very same views, since they apparently took the anus as the center and stronghold of decay. Worry about intestinal decay eventually evolved into something of a national concern. It seems to have governed daily life even in the time of Herodotus, who wrote: "For three consecutive days in every month they purge themselves, pursuing after health by means of emetics and drenches; for they think it is from the food they eat that all sicknesses come to men."

To live by this notion must have been rather uncomfortable for the average Egyptian. Doomed to walk around all day with an internal load of deadly material, the Egyptians took whatever measures were necessary. In doing so, they became the world's foremost experts on enemas. Their enormous pharmacopoeia (close to 700 items) may be almost worthless by modern standards, but there was one effect it could definitely induce, either a hearty bowel movement or immediate diarrhea.

According to former Harvard Medical School pathologist, Guido Majno, M.D., the worst thing feared by the ancient Egyptians was something dreadful lurking in their bowels called *ukhedu*. His classic work, *The Healing Hand-Man and Wound in the Ancient World* explained it in detail. This ukhedu, he noted, lay quite dormant but could travel elsewhere in the body if it so chose to do. The rough translation of ukhedu means "rotten stuff par excellence." It could be either male or female and cause considerable pain and sickness, but with the proper remedies could be destroyed.

Ukhedu was thought to work its way through the blood vessels from its origin within the colon, setting up disease as it went along. Thus, what bacteria now does, ukhedu once did. Today a few medical journals have subscribed to near similar views for the likely causes of most illnesses. For instance, *Archives of Physical Therapy* 17:154-61, (1936) noted: the colon is a common center of infection and its lumen a breeding place for many bacteria. Toxins, native proteins and bacteria readily pass through the intact mucous membrane of the colon and are taken up by the capillaries and lymphatics.

The procedure for administering an enema is relatively simple. The first thing is to be as relaxed as possible while taking one. This can be achieved by listening to music with soft, easy sounds to it before and during the taking of an enema. This is what the ancient Maya did when they took their own hallucinogenic enemas, reported the authors of *Maya Ruins in Central America in Color*. Among the musical instruments which they employed for creating such easy-listening sounds were horns, trumpets, flutes, drums, tom toms, rattles, and carapaces (hollow turtle shells). Certain wall murals in some Classic Maya tombs in the Peten area of Guatemala, depict an enema being accompanied by a musical band playing with a carapace, rattles, tom toms, and flutes. Maybe a little bit of Beethoven's incredibly relaxing "Pastoral Symphony" might be appropriate here.

Then comes the enema itself. Usually somewhere between one to two pints of liquid solution is sufficient for the average enema. However, if several are to be given in succession, then this amount should obviously be decreased. Generally, no more than three enemas ought to be administered at any given time, because of the fatiguing results which they can produce, not to mention depleting the body of many valuable nutrients as well (particularly calcium, magnesium, and potassium). An enema will be more effective, reported the May 1977 *American Journal of Nursing* if the patient is thoroughly relaxed and retains the fluid for at least five minutes.

Our Anthropological Research Center here in Salt Lake City conducted a somewhat informal survey a few years back with a local colonic therapist. We wanted to see just how responsive people would be to enemas in stressful and unstressed environments. Two groups of five volunteers, each consisting of three men and two women between the ages of 37 and 55, were given enemas at separate intervals on different days. Group A received their enemas in a deliberately staged hectic and noisy environment, with the result that it required multiple enemas for four of them to completely evacuate their bowels of all existing fecal material. On the other hand, Group B received their enemas in relaxed surroundings with soft lights, pastel wall colors, and easy-listening music. Four of the five experienced nearly complete evacuations of accumulated feces from their bowels with just one enema, while only one individual required an additional second enema to do the job thoroughly. Also Group B participants were able to hold their enema solutions longer (an average of 6.1 minutes) than did Group A (an average of just 3.2 minutes).

The temperature of the enema solution ought to be comfortably warm (about 105 degrees F). If it's hot, one might seriously damage his or her intestinal mucosa; if too cold, on the other hand, it might cause unnecessary cramping. Since the hand can tolerate more heat than mucous membrane can, this might not be too reliable as a way of testing the proper temperature of the solution itself.

The left side is the best position to lie in with the right knee flexed, when taking an enema. This promotes flow into the sigmoid and descending colon. The person should then turn on his or her right side while still in a prone position and retaining the enema solution.

This may help the solution flow into the transverse and ascending portions of the colon and provide for a more thorough cleansing of the intestinal tract. In other situations, knee-chest positions while lying down may be necessary when taking an enema.

The end of the syringe should be lubricated with something like vaseline, olive oil, or even some of your own saliva. It is then inserted into the rectum with a slight turning motion at an angle pointing toward the person's belly button. The syringe should go in no further than three inches. If several deep breaths are taken during, insertion, the anal sphincter relaxes more as the syringe is slowly, gently, and carefully slid into the anus.

Because the enema solution flows by gravity, the elevation of the enema receptacle is important. A foot above a prone-positioned body on the floor or two feet above a mattress is suggested. If the enema fluid doesn't flow freely, the end of the rectal tube should be checked for possible fecal occlusion. If this is the case, remove the tube, clean the tip, and start the solution flowing again as soon as the tube is reinserted.

A Healthy Regard for the Liver

In diverse parts of the ancient world, the liver occupied a central position in superstitious or mystical beliefs about man's character and destiny. In Babylon during the second millennium B.C., the soul was thought to reside in the liver, and sheep livers were used for divination and prophecy. In the *Bible* (Ezekiel 21:21) it's reported that "...the king of Babylon stood at the parting of the ways, at the head of the two ways, to use divination: he made his arrows bright, he consulted with images, he looked in the liver."

The most common animals used for sacrificial purposes in Babylon and Assyria were sheep. In order to learn the will of the gods whom they worshipped daily, these ancient cultures would kill a sheep and promptly examine its liver while still warm and fresh. According to symptoms discovered on the liver, certain conclusions could be made relative to the observed signs. If they looked favorable, then an undertaking could be commenced at once; if not so favorable, the action would be postponed until a later time.

The most perfect liver inspection (or hepatoscopy) was when the organ of the sacrificial sheep became one with the spirit of the god (or gods) then being worshipped. The animal's liver could then reflect the disposition and will of said deity in much the same manner as man might view his image in a mirror.

This particular type of organ divination later evolved into a rather elaborate pseudoscience of its own, for which there were a number of different specialists, since no two livers were ever exactly alike. At the close of the Babylonian empire, the practice spread to other lands.

In conjunction with the liver, other things were studied with equal intensity. Temple priests paid close attention to the appearance of an animal's gall, and to the various lobes of the gall bladder and of the gall ducts of both the large and small appendices to the liver and its veins.

In some ways such practices compared favorably with the science of astrology, then employed concurrent with the former as men attempted to learn more about what their gods were thinking and feeling. Thus, internal organs like the liver and gall bladder were equated in importance to the stars that shone at night in ancient times. If people *then* held such regard for something as vital as the liver, shouldn't we show it greater respect today in terms of better health care for it?

Some medical evidence which has surfaced in this century, shows that the Babylonians weren't entirely wrong in assuming that the liver was the seat of life or place where the soul and its emotions resided. According to the January 1924 *Proceedings of the Society for Experimental Biology and Medicine,* the liver contributes towards the chemical regulation of the heart beat and could in some other ways be connected therewith in a social sense of the word. The fluid which has passed the liver contains something which has an augmentor action on the heart and decreases the inhibitory action of the vagi. The liver contributes towards the chemical regulation of the heart beat, acting on the neuromuscular mechanisms of the heart.

Also, a somewhat later journal, the January 1956 issue of *Modern Concepts of Cardiovascular Disease* pointed out that corollary damage to the liver always seems to lead to a corresponding incidence of congestive heart failure as well. The connection between the two wasn't as fully understood as doctors hoped it might be, but what had become clear in their own minds from the research data available then was that the health of the liver and the condition of the heart were *inseparably* connected: when one suffered so did the other, and vice-versa.

If we can accept the generally understood philosophical principle that from our hearts come various feelings, then it isn't too difficult to imagine the liver as also playing a role in forming our emotions. Secondly, the involvement of the liver in strong emotions, are found in many Indo-European languages, modern, medieval, and ancient, according to Sherman M. Mellinkoff, M.D. in *Gastroenterology* 76:636—38, (1979).

This linguistic connection, together with the hormonal regulation of the heart beat by the liver, adds further credence to these old Babylonian beliefs that the life and soul of man were invariably tied up with the liver. In ancient Akkadian texts, for example, there is this phrase: "may your angry heart quiet down, may your liver relax;" and another, "may your heart be pleased, may your liver be happy." Similarly, in a very old Hittite text appears this phrase, "let them soften your heart and let them pacify your liver." In fact, as Dr. Mellinkoff observes in his remarkable article, some Semitic languages draw "a clear relationship between bile and emotion."

And, as if this were not enough proof, one only needs to look into Oriental medicine to find numerous references to the gall bladder and the liver as influencing human emotions. The Japanese speak of a man with "a hefty liver" (kimo ga futoi) as bold and daring. In Chinese, the term for liver is "kan" and for gall it is "tan."

"Tan" is generally synonymous with courage; "mei yoyuu tantzu" literally means having no gall, and approximates the American equivalent of "no guts." "Kan" may be perceived as the seat of emotion along with the heart. Thus, one who is heartless has no heart-liver ("hsin-kan"). Yet the same liver connotes anger in "kan huo" (liver-fire). Both "liver-vapor" (tan-chi) and "liver-gall" (kan-tan) mean courage. Since ancient times (perhaps 2,000 years ago) in China, "tasting the gall" has signified nursing a grievance and a desire for revenge.

Even in parts of Africa, there exist related connections between the liver and human emotions. In Kpelle, for instance (where a Southwestern hionde language is spoken) "his liver has lain clown" (nu aa aa) means "he is satisfied, pleased." Some other Kpelle expressions implicating the liver in the emotions are as follows: "His liver hurts" (He is sad), "his liver tastes good" (he is happy), "their livers sat down" (they are at peace), "his liver is white" (he feels good will). Other African languages in which similar expressions are found include Akan Fante, Asante, and Tivi (of Ghana) and Efik (of southwestern Nigeria).

Some African tribes still worship the liver as the habitation for the soul in modern times. In Dr. Price's classic work *Nutrition and Physical Degeneration*, he cites the tall Neurs as but one example of this custom. They have a belief which to them is their religion that every man and woman has a soul which resides in the liver and that a man's character and physical growth depend upon how well he feeds that soul by eating the livers of animals. The liver is so sacred that it may not be touched by human hands. It is always handled with their spear or saber, or with specially prepared forked sticks. It is eaten both raw and cooked.

In his *Gastroenterology* report cited earlier, Mellinkoff wondered why, in so many different unrelated languages, do words for bile, liver, and gall bladder signify qualities of mood or character, especially degrees of courage, anger, equanimity, depression, or contentment. Surely, he reasoned, the liver has held an important place in human lives from the Babylonian period to the Middle Ages.

Biological Functions of the Liver

But by Mellinkoff's own admission, his conclusions are only *part* of the answer as to why ancient man believed that mood or character emanated from the liver. The other reason may lay in important biological function of this organ for the rest of the body. In one of the most interesting articles l have ever read on the liver, science writer Ron Kotulak, lists three primary functions of this organ that are *absolutely essential* to the life of the body. His observations were taken from the November 8th, 1978 issue of the *Chicago Tribune* (Sec. 2, pp. 1;15). I have summarized them as follows:

1. The liver makes proteins from nutrients absorbed from the small intestine and sends them all over the body to build cells.

2. The sugar you eat goes to the liver where it is stored as glycogen. When you need energy, the liver frees the glycogen and converts it back into sugar. That's why heavy drinkers often are fatigued. Alcohol impairs the liver and impedes its energy production.

3. The liver plays a *vital* role in maintaining the "aliveness" of the brain. Medical researchers do not know how the liver keeps the brain alert. But they do know that when the liver malfunctions the brain quickly shuts down.

Nearly everyone has heard of the medical condition called hypoglycemia or low blood sugar. It is not my intention here to discuss all of its medical ramifications. Suffice it to say, though, some physicians have linked this particular problem to a gradual deterioration of the health of the liver, as well as the more commonly blamed breakdown of the pancreas.

Harry Salzer, M.D., a psychiatrist, was one of the first to make a distinct connection between liver disturbances and hypoglycemia. In 1965, he delivered a paper on hypoglycemia at the annual convention of the National Medical Association in which he reported on the 36 major psychiatric, somatic, and neurologic symptoms of 300 hypoglycemia patients. His paper, "Relative Hypoglycemia as a Cause of Neuropsychiatric Illness," was later published in the *Journal of the National Medical Association* 58:12-17, (1966).

As one follows his list of symptoms usually associated with hypoglycemia, one is impressed with the fact that at least one-third of them have to do with irrational mood or character behaviors. Could this not then suggest that the Babylonians were probably right after all in assuming that the liver directly affected our emotions? Salzer's list of symptoms for hypoglycemia are as follows:

(1) *psychiatric:* depression, insomnia, anxiety, irritability, crying spells, phobias, lack of concentration, forgetfulness or confusion, unsocial or antisocial behavior, restlessness, previous psychosis, and suicidal tendencies:

(2) *somatic:* exhaustion or fatigue, sweating, tachycardia, anorexia, chronic ingestion or bloating, cold hands or feet, joint pains, obesity, and abdominal spasm; and

(3) *neurologic:* headache, tremors, muscle pains and backaches, numbness, muscular twitching or cramps, staggering, fainting or blackouts, and convulsions.

Hence, as we try to find some other underlying reason for man's early belief in the liver being the seat of life, besides the religious mysticism once attached to it, we are more inclined to the blood sugar role it plays as a second, more sensible explanation to this organ's involvement with human emotions. If the liver is unable to release adequate glycogen for conversion back into blood sugar, then the brains alert activities quickly diminish. Once this transpires, then other vital parts of the body wired directly to the brain, such as the central nervous system and the heart, soon suffer as well. In no time at all, the entire body feels generally crummy and with it come lousy feelings and bad thoughts. All of this pretty much resulting from the liver's inability to store and release sugar, "the fuel of life," in the form of glycogen. With this alternative view in mind, it isn't so difficult to understand how easily the Babylonians and others could associate the liver with human emotions.

Other important functions of the liver not previously cited are as follows:

(1). It produces bile, and through the bile salts contained in this digestive secretion it facilitates the absorption of fat and fat-soluble vitamins.

(2). The liver produces a large number of proteins and is the site of synthesis of all plasma proteins except the immunoglobulins. Of the hepatic proteins, albumin (also in the white of an egg) is the most important; 10 to 15 grams of albumin are synthesized in the liver per day. The liver is also the site of production of important binding globulins such as that which binds iron, copper, and various combinations of globulin and lipid called lipoproteins. Additionally, the liver is the site of production of the proteins concerned in blood coagulation and of amino-acid degradation to alpha-keto-acids and ammonia. Ammonia is then converted in the liver to urea by a series of enzymes acting in the Krebs urea cycle.

(3). The liver plays an essential role in fat metabolism. It's able to utilize free fatty acids released from fat deposits in order to provide energy. It also converts free fatty acids to triglyceride and other lipids. The normal liver contains fat, usually about 5% of its weight. In certain circumstances, such as diabetes, starvation, and alcoholic liver disease this amount is much increased.

(4). The liver also plays a central role in the breakdown of steroid hormones such as cortisol, testosterone, and estrogen. These hormones undergo degradation, conjugation, and excretion in the bile. Antidiuretic hormone is also removed from the circulation by the liver. Many drugs are also altered by the liver so that they become more water soluble and can hence be excreted in the urine. An important system of enzymes exists in the smooth endoplasmic reticulum which is responsible for much of this function. Known as the microsomal enzyme system by many scientists, this drug-metabolizing assemblage can be altered by drugs so that an increased or decreased concentration of enzyme may result. It has been shown, for instance, that barbiturates are very potent inducers of the enzymes responsible for the conjugation of bilirubin (a red-colored bile).

(5). The liver also has important storage functions and among the substances stored are iron, vitamin B_{12}, and folic acid. The amount of B_{12} stored in the liver is sufficient to last some two to three years even if B_{12} absorption fails completely.

(6). The detoxification of most of the environmental pollutants we absorb into our bodies takes place in the liver. Because the liver removes harmful chemicals and destroys various parasites conveyed into the body, it may become severely weakened itself. That is why persons who have suffered malaria, dysentery, and other bacterial diseases, or have been accidentally poisoned by chemicals, may also have liver diseases. Certain organs necessary for the elimination of such toxins from the body, in fact, are thought to be tied in somehow with the liver. As the South American medical journal, *Acta Physiologica Latino Americana* 10:179-81, (1960) noted, the liver can produce both diuretic and antidiuretic hormones which affects urinary output to quite a degree.

Not bad for a soft, smooth, football-size organ that performs at least 5,000 different biochemical reactions throughout the body! Held in place by five ligaments just under the strong muscular diaphragm and bony support of the lower rib cage, it weighs between 3 to 4 pounds and is the most solid organ inside the body. It is also the only organ capable of regenerating itself if a substantial portion is surgically removed! If this dark red or chocolate-colored mass ever ceased functioning, you wouldn't be able to live more than 8 to 24 hours at the most! This highly complicated organ is actually an extremely versatile chemical laboratory which performs hundreds of intricate biological functions necessary for the maintenance of *your life!*

Although some of its better and lesser known functions have already been cited, yet one more remains as a prime example of the myriad things it can do, which would never occur to most of us. Do you know that this organ, sitting principally on the right side of your abdominal cavity, controls to a large extent your appetite and taste for food? While sounding somewhat far-fetched to the unlearned, yet this is a proven, scientific fact!

As the November, 1985 *American Journal of Clinical Nutrition* pointed out, information about liver metabolism is transmitted to areas in the brain which receive other information connected to feeding such as from gustatory and central glucoreceptors. The liver is probably important in controlling feeding as part of a sequence of integrated events beginning in the mouth, integrated by the brain, and ending with the appropriate behaviors.

Ways to Tonify the Liver

There are a number of ways to tonify the liver. One is by *thinking good thoughts*. A colleague of mine, California practicing folk herbalist, Michael Tierra, stated in the June, 1988 issue of *East West* health journal that negative feelings and thoughts can produce hormonal reactions harmful to the liver. For instance, someone who is easily angered has an adrenalin rush each time he gets upset. This constant release of internal toxins further burdens the liver. If the anger persists—especially if there is also overeating and too much fatty, oily food—the liver becomes overtaxed and begins to function improperly, sometimes resulting in allergic tendencies.

A large number of natural foods, herbs, and nutritional supplements will also be of definite assistance in helping the liver to regain its former energy and strength. They are included below with the appropriate references following each entry and available sources:

ARNICA (Arnica montana): Experiments conducted by Soviet scientists on rats with toxic liver injury induced by carbon tetrachloride have shown that the preparation presenting a sum of phenolic compounds of A. montana and foliated Arnica seems to favor a more completed recovery of the bile secretion intensity, synthesis, and excretion of bile acids and bilirubin (red bile), and cholesterol. It also accelerates the recovery of activity of serum enzymes. S.M. Marchishin, "Efficacy of phenolic compounds of Arnica in toxic liver injury." *Farmakologiia I Toksikologiia*, pp. 102-106 (June, 1982). (An extract of arnica flowers and root and an oil extract of arnica flowers is available from Eclectic Institute, Portland, Oregon.)

BEET (Beta vulgaris): Dr. Alexander Ferenczi treated a variety of cancers with organic beet juice and beet juice powder at a hospital in Csoma, Hungary between 1955-1959. Of 22 patients who tolerated beet therapy, 21 of them experienced varying degrees of improvement as demonstrated by shrinking of their tumors, noticeable weight gains, decreased ESR, and definite improvements in appetite and general health. A skin cancer was even successfully treated with concentrated beet juice compresses. In rats inoculated with Guerin tumors, the lifespan of those whose diet was supplemented with beet root was 20% longer than that of controls. Dr. Ferenczi attributed the antitumor activity in beets to their 'red coloring matter' or betalains. (R. A. Buist, "Beet root as cancer therapy." *International Clinical Nutrition Review* 6:107-112, July, 1986).

BREWER'S YEAST/B-COMPLEX VITAMINS: For years the food industry has been permitted to use various oil-soluble coal-tar dyes in coloring oils, oleomargarine, and other vegetable fat substitutes for butter. Among these has been dimethyl-amino-azobenzene, commercially known as butter-yellow. Now this particular coal-tar dye is highly active in producing liver cancer in rats. Several groups of albino rats were fed butter-yellow in an olive oil-rice mixture. Some groups had supplements of brewer's yeast given them, while others did not. Those *without* the brewer's yeast experienced a lot of liver cancer; but the yeast-fed rodents showed *very low* incidence of liver cancer (K. Sugiura and C.P. Rhoads, M.D. "Experimental liver cancer in rats and its inhibition by rice-bran extract, yeast, and yeast extract." *Cancer Research* 1:3-16, 1941). Another study showed that obese people have strong evidence of liver disease. But when put on a reducing program consisting of a high-protein diet supplemented by choline and vitamins of the B-complex group, liver regeneration and further preventing of liver damage became readily apparent (Samuel Zelman, M.D., "The liver in obesity." *AMA Archives of Internal Medicine* 90:141-56, 1952). (Quest Vitamins of Vancouver, B.C. makes available high-quality, hypoallergenic Choline Tablets (250 mg.), Mega B-100 (Timed Release Tablets), and Brewer's Yeast Tablets in some American health food stores and nutrition centers).

CRANBERRIES (Vaccinium macrocarpum): Cranberry juice has been recognized by many urologists as being able to prevent infectious bacteria from adhering to the urinary tract. (1) This wonderful antibacterial action is due to hippuric acid, which is formed after whole cranberries or cranberry juice is consumed. (2) Nearly all of the conversion, however, takes place in the liver. The trace amounts of quinic acid in cranberries are first transformed to benzoic and finally to hippuric acid. But in transforming benzoic acid into hippuric acid, glycine is required, which is largely synthesized by the liver. Hence, cranberries and cranberry juice would be good for the liver as well as the urinary tract itself.

1. A. E. Sobota, "Inhibition of bacterial adherence by cranberry juice: potential use for the treatment of urinary tract infections." *Journal of Urology* 131:1013-16, (May, 1984).

2. P.T. Bodel, M.D., et al., "Cranberry juice and the antibacterial action of hippuric acid." *Journal of Laboratory and Clinical Medicine* 54:881-87, (Dec. ,1959).

3. C.R. Fellers, et al., "Effect of cranberries on urinary acidity and blood alkali reserve." *Journal of Nutrition* 6:455-63, (Sept., 1933).

Two exceptional sources for powdered cranberry are Michael's Health Products of San Antonio, Texas and Murdock Pharmaceutical of Springville, Utah. In fact, a nutritional and organic acid analysis was made of cranberry juice cocktail and Murdock's own Cranberry Powder U T. Quinic acid, an important antibacterial substance in cranberries, was found to be present in 100 grams of juice cocktail in just trace amounts [0.26%]; while in Murdock's encapsulated product per 100 grams of powder it was present in much higher quantities [7.24%]. This suggests that Murdock's Cranberry Juice Powder U. T. Nature's Way Cranberry Powder is much better to take than ordinary cranberry juice cocktail would be. The results of this analysis were reported to the Symposium on Advances in Clinical Nutrition at the American College of Nutrition's 29th Annual Meeting in New Orleans, September 14-16, 1988.

DANDELION (Taraxacum officinale): An Austrian Catholic nun, who specialized in herbal therapy, said this herb is useful in disorders of the liver and of the gall bladder. In Yugoslavia she noticed the guests received a small bowl of dandelion greens besides the fresh salads. Asked why, the physician, a well-known liver specialist, told her dandelion has a beneficial effect on the liver. People who feel constantly tired and are without energy should take a 14-day course of treatment with the fresh stems of dandelion. (M. Treben. *Health Through God's Pharmacy*; Austria, 1984, p. 23).

Dandelion may be gathered fresh from lawns, meadows, and pastures. However care must be taken to harvest it from unsprayed fields and *never* from the sides of public highways or railroad tracks, where much spraying is done to keep the weeds down. An excellent herbal formula for the liver, Q_{13}, has dandelion in it and is available through the American branch of Quest Vitamins of Vancouver, B.C. or in some larger health food stores. Also, a most excellent tasting and very nutritive coffee substitute beverage with lots of dandelion in it is available from Michael's Health Products of San Antonio, Texas.

VITAMIN E: Partially hepatectomized (liver surgically removed) rats were fed a dietary vitamin E (DL-alpha-tocopheryl acetate). A (40 mg/kg diet) resulted in an increase in liver regeneration as compared to a similar control group that was vitamin E-deficient. (V.C. gavino, et al., "Effect of dietary vitamin E and Santoquin on regenerating rat liver." *Life Sciences* 36:1771-77, May 6, 1985). (Quest Vitamins of Vancouver, B.C. has made available to its U.S. and Canadian markets varying potencies of high-grade d-alpha tocopherol distilled from soya bean oil. Quest's Vitamin E comes in

100 l.U., 200 l.U., 400 l.U. or 1,000 l.U. strengths).

LEMON JUICE (Citrus limon): The late, renowned nutritionist Paavo Airola recommended a special liver detoxifying juice fast for three days to treat congested, clogged, and toxic liver conditions. Mix fresh juice of ten lemons in two quarts of water, sweetened with natural honey. Drink one glass every two hours. Also, twice daily drink a green vegetable juice mixed with 50% beet juice. Another popular liver cleansing method is as follows: On two evenings, take one cup of equal parts fresh lemon juice and olive oil (approximately two ounces each). On the third evening take a double dose (four ounces of each). On the following morning, take an enema. Follow it with a second enema to which one cup freshly brewed coffee has been added. Retain the coffee enema for at least 20 minutes. (P. Airola. *How to Get Well;* Phoenix, 1976; pp.122-23). (Lemons are available from any local supermarket. Bottled lemon juice, such as ReaLemon, may also be used).

MILK THISTLE SEED (Silbyum marianum): A West German pharmacologist, G. Vogel, discovered that the three flavanolignans (silybin, silydianin, and silychristin) in the seeds (collectively called silymarin) helps to protect the liver against certain deadly chemical toxins. These would include the amatoxins, phalloidine, and amanitine found in the death-cap toadstool, as well as other deadly man made chemicals lurking in our environment today. (G. Vogel, "Natural substances with effects on the liver." In H. Wagner's and P. Wolff's, *New Natural Products and Plant Drugs with Pharmacological, Biological or Therapeutical Activity;* New York, 1977; pp. 249-65). (Nature's Way of Springville, Utah distributes a highly-concentrated form of silymarin from West Germany in the United States in a product called Thisilyn).

PROTEIN: The late nutritional authority, Dr. Paavo Airola recommended that high quality proteins be included in the diets of those suffering from liver disorders to expedite their recoveries. (P. Airola. *How to Get Well;* Phoenix, 1976; p. 123). Quest Vitamins of Vancouver, B.C. manufactures a Super Protein formula which is entirely agreeable with nearly all digestive systems. The amino acid profile in Super Protein exceeds in every category the ideal standard established by the joint FAO/ World Health Organization Committee in 1965. (See "Protein Requirements," Tech Report 301, WHO, Geneva, Switzerland). Super Protein is unique in that it contains a high content of egg albumin. Albumin is the most important liver protein, with up to 15 grams being synthesized by the liver each day. Super Protein is ideal for giving new vitality and strength to nutritionally depleted livers.

SAGE (Salvia miltiorrhiza): Research conducted at the Shanxi Medical College in mainland China confirms the value of sage in liver regeneration. This species of sage, along with safflower, tangkuei (or dongquai), and peach were observed in albino rats which had had their middle and left liver lobes surgically removed. The rodents were then divided into five groups, one control group and four drug groups, with each of the aforementioned herbs being given twice after the operation. Two days later, all rats were autopsied with a piece of liver tissue taken from each animal for histological survey and serum isolated for biochemical tests. The rats given sage experienced accelerated hepatic regeneration over the other groups on the rest of the above herbs (Ma Xuehui, "Effect of Salvia miltiorrhiza on experimental hepatic regeneration." *Chung Hsi I Chih Ho Tsa Chih* 3:180-81, 1983). (Only Quest Vitamins of Vancouver, O.C. has made a unique liver regenerating formula, Q_{37}, which includes not only sage, safflower, tangkuei, and peach leaves, but also tomato seed powder, another great liver regenerator.)

TANNIC ACID: Studies by Japanese scientists shows that the tannins occurring in many medicinal plants are effective against diseases such as liver injury and arteriosclerosis. (T. Okuda, et al., "Studies on the activities of tannins and related compounds from medicinal plants and drugs. Inhibitory effects on lipid peroxidation in mitochondria and microsomes of liver." *Chemical and Pharmaceutical Bulletin* 31:1625, 1983). Herbs such as white oak bark, chicory root, the mints, wild Oregon grape root, uva ursi, and hops contain varying amounts of tarinic acid.

TOMATO JUICE (Lycopersicon esculentum): Clinical studies conducted at Tohoku University in Sendai, Japan showed that glycogen formation in the liver was greatly accelerated when this fresh vegetable juice was administered to rabbits. An admixture of vitamins C, P, and K were believed to be responsible for this activity. Tomato juice is effective clinically in improving liver disturbance and, according to a published medical report, exercising a good influence on the detoxicating (detoxifying) function of the liver. (Y. Tohuoka, "Experimental studies on treatment for liver disturbances." *Tohoku Journal of Experimental Medicine* 57:343-48, 1953). I have found that an eight-ounce glass of Campbell's sodium-free tomato juice with one tablespoon of lemon juice added is great for refreshing the liver and giving the body a needed boost of energy. Sodium-free V-8 Juice is also good for this. For a really terrific liver energizer, try mixing equal parts (in thirds) of tomato, carrot, and mixed green juices together and drink an eight or ten ounce glass of the same with some lemon or lime juice added for zest. There's nothing quite like it! And surprisingly, this concoction really gives the body an energy lift! Quest Vitamins' herbal Q_{37} formula for liver regeneration includes tomato seed powder).

WORMWOOD (Artemisia species): Analysis of an extract of a species of wormwood (A. capillaris) buds indicates that a number of existing flavonoids and a coumarin protect the liver against certain chemically-induced lesions (Y. Kiso, et al., "Antihepatotoxic principles of A. capillaris buds." *Planta Medica* 37:81, 1984). (Wormwood can be taken in tea or capsule form for this).

ZUCCHINI SQUASH (Cucurbita pepo): A famous American medical doctor who treated thousands of his patients with prescriptions of food instead of drugs, strongly recommended zucchini for tonifying the liver. In his national best-seller, *Food is Your Best Medicine* (N.Y., 1976; pp. 64;204;210; 217), Henry G. Beer, M.D. said sodium is the most important alkaline element in the body. The liver is the richest of all the organs in sodium, its chief chemical element. Therefore, as the largest storehouse of sodium the liver is the body's second line of defense against infections. When the liver is depleted of sodium in order to neutralize its acids, its functions may be so severely inhibited that illness results. If the liver could keep the blood stream clean by filtering out damaging poisons, man could live indefinitely, barring physical accidents. Dietetic histories point out that for hundreds of years, the Italians used zucchini as a cure-all. The zucchini is an especially sodium-rich vegetable, as are other members of the squash-cucumber-melon family. If you wish to know the condition of your liver, he advised, then just study the tongue's coating and papillae closely. Secondly, he recognized that chronic fatigue is one of the first symptoms of liver impairment. For this he suggested, sodium-rich vegetable and brewer's yeast.

CHAPTER THREE

ANCIENT BABYLONIAN DIVINING
FOR MODERN HEALTH PROBLEMS

Divining for Health Reasons

In the previous chapter there was a lengthy discussion on hepatoscopy or liver inspection. The ancient Babylonians resorted to
this practice often with the internal organs of freshly sacrificed
lambs in order to learn the mind and will of the gods concerning
them in routine and extraordinary daily affairs of life. But divining was also used for ascertaining a person's state of health, with
one of the most popular forms for this being astrology. A general
explanation of the art of divining may be helpful for the reader first
of all, before details on the other are given.

The importance of divination in Mesopotamian civilization is
emphasized by the large number of omen collections and related
cuneiform (wedge-shaped writing) texts that have been preserved.
Such texts range in time from the late (post-Hammurabi) Old Babylonian period up to the time of the Selecid kings, offering us an
abundance of material concerning various techniques of divination.

Moreover, allusions to divination practices abound in historical
and religious literature. There can be little doubt in any scholar's
mind that Akkadian divination—all extant texts are written in
that language—was considered a major intellectual achievement in
Mesopotamia and surrounding countries.

Basically, Babylonian divination represented a technique of
communication with the supernatural forces that were supposed to
have shaped the history of the individual as well as that of a group.
It presupposed the belief that these powers were able and, at times,
often willing to communicate their intentions and that they were
interested in the well-being of the individual or the group. In other
words, if evil was to be predicted or threatened by chance, it could be
averted through appropriate means.

Thus, if an individual were to be strickened with a particular
malady, he or she could call upon the temple diviner and inquire as
to any possible changes in his or her state of health for the immediate future. And then, if through the divining art something unpleasant was portrayed, the person on whom this affliction might

fall, could appeal to the gods through the diviner for means and ways to avoid contracting this or that illness.

Contact or communication with such heavenly powers was established in several ways. The deity being petitioned could either answer questions put to him or, of his own accord, attempt to communicate in whatever medium he found acceptable. Such two-way communication required a special technique. In fact, two techniques were known in ancient Babylon: an operational one and a magical kind. In both instances, the answer came forth in two possible manners: one was binary, that is, a yes-or-no answer; the other was based on a code accepted by both the deity and the diviner.

The fact that Mesopotamian divination underwent a complex historical development should not be overlooked. Not only did emphasis and preferences change in the course of time, but the methods also differed from time to time and region to region. Equally important was the diversity of methods, based on social status. There were practices for the king, others to which the poor often resorted, native practices, and those that were imported from abroad.

In operational divination, the temple diviner offered a specific deity the opportunity of directly affecting an object activated by the diviner himself, as in the casting of lots, in the pouring of oil into water, or in producing smoke from a censer. The deity had the power to manipulate the lots, affect the spreading of oil, and change the shape of ascending smoke in order to communicate. In the last example of rising smoke, we find a certain similarity here with that of the old Native American Indian custom of watching for the Great Spirit's response in campfire smoke.

In what is termed a magical technique, the deity produced changes in natural phenomena, such as wind, thunder, and the movement of the stars, or affected the behavior or the external or internal (liver, gall bladder) features of animals and even of human beings. Here again, one may find a dichotomy of sorts: the acts of the god being petitioned at the time could be provoked or unprovoked as it were. To provoke a response from a deity, a magical act of the diviner probably singled out certain areas within his range of understanding in which he expected the deity to react in answer to his specific question. The deity was provided a certain setting and a given time in which to communicate.

Of the three operational practices mentioned so far, the throwing of lots and the observation of oil in water (lecanomancy) will be treated here, since so little is known about the last, the observation of smoke from incense (libanomancy), only that it once existed in ancient Babylon.

The first technique had no cultic status in Mesopotamia, but was frequently used on a daily basis in many mundane affairs. We know from legal documents that in the Old Babylonian period and in Susa lots were used to assign the shares of an estate to the sons. We learn from later documents that shares of temple income were originally distributed by lot to certain officials of the sanctuary. In these instances, the throwing of lots—marked sticks of wood—established a sequence among persons of equal status that would be acceptable, as divinely ordained, to all participants. This was also the case with the Assyrian custom used to select the official who was to give his name to the new year by means of clay dice. An isolated text from Assur spoke of the use of two stone lots, apparently furnishing positive or negative answers to health questions. There is a bit more evidence from Boghazkeui. A small group of omen texts, written characteristically in Hittite, spoke of divination by means of lots. The Hittite and the Assyrian evidence suggests the possibility of a substratum influence in this type of divination.

An interesting practice along the lines of casting lots, for which no documentation in the Mesopotamian cuneiform texts exists, is cited in Ezekiel 21:21 (which was mentioned in the previous chapter). Here reference is made to a king of Babylon using arrows and examining a sacrificed lamb's liver to determine in which direction he ought to go either "at the parting of the way, [or] at the head of two ways."

Now lest those of Christian persuasion denounce such a thing as devilish, let me remind them that the god of the Hebrews, Jehovah, frequently worked through the casting of lots to accomplish His own will and purposes among His chosen people. The *Bible* is replete with instances of this. The use of the lot to determine doubtful questions was much in vogue among ancient Israel (Esther 3:7; Jonah 1:7; Matthew 27: 35). Stones or inscribed tablets, or the like, were put into a common vessel and, having been shaken, were drawn out or cast upon the ground or some level surface. The act was generally preceded by prayer and was a direct appeal to God to decide the matter by influencing whichever way the lots would fall. Nowhere is there better evidence of this than in The Acts of the Apostles 1:23-26, wherein Matthias was chosen to fill the vacancy of the late Judas over that of Barnabas: "And they gave forth their lots; and the lot fell upon Matthias; and he was numbered with the [other] eleven apostles."

Even today, among some groups of conservative practicing Christians, the casting of lots is still used. As an anthropologist, I have studied and evaluated the unique communal culture of the Hutterian Brethren colonies scattered throughout Montana, the

Dakotas and western Canada. These Anabaptists, who are doctrinally similar to the old-order Amish and Mennonite communities of the Americas, select their new ministers and determine how a colony will be split when it's ready to divide, by the simple casting of lots and prayers before and after this practice. So how can anyone dare to criticize such a thing as not being ordained of Heaven for wise and good purposes?

In the early history of the Jewish people, God was pleased to use the lot as a method of making known his will. The weighty statement was made in Proverbs 16:33, "The lot is cast into the lap; but the whole disposing thereof is of the Lord." The land of Canaan was divided among the twelve tribes by Lot (Joshua 14:2;18:6). And upon one occasion, Saul and Jonathan stood on one side and Jonathan cast lots against the people. The king and his son being thus singled out, they cast lots with each other, Jonathan being finally pointed out by this method of inquiry (1 Samuel 14:40-45). The courses of the priests were settled by lot (1 Chronicle 24:5). Thus, by the casting of lots were the ancient Israelites able to discern the will of God in many useful and important things.

But it's equally interesting to observe that after the Holy Ghost had fallen upon the twelve apostles of Christ, that they no longer needed to rely upon the casting of lots anymore to reach particular decisions. Instead, their answers came by way of divine revelation or inspiration. We can see that the casting of lots is more for those who's own intuitive powers of personal revelation haven't been fully developed yet.

With regard to lecanomancy, a different kind of interpretation was used. The diviner, who was called baru, poured oil into a bowl of water which he held in his lap. This was done to establish the will of the deity, either with regard to the country or to an individual. The movements of the oil in the water, in relation to the surface or to the rim of the cup, could portend for the king peace and prosperity or war and rebellion; for the private citizen it could portend progeny, success in business, the recovery of health, the right girl he was about to marry, or just the opposite of all these things. Three Old Babylonian tablets were discovered many years ago that contain omens dealing with this particular type of divination, which apparently went out of use in a later period.

How to Cast Lots and Interpret Correctly for Personal Health Knowledge

It's interesting to consider that the casting of lots in ancient times for information about personal matters, took precedent over other forms of supernatural communication. In fact, from the scant evidence available, it seems that the present ouji board would have been outlawed or viewed with a certain apprehension in Mesopotamian times. Hence, if the individual reader is unable to receive divine communication from legitimate sources through the mediums of prayers and personal revelation, then the use of lots is helpful, provided it's preceded by and concluded with sincere prayers of faith, hope, and good will.

A person can procure from any wood shop, mill, or lumber yard small bits of wood no more than two inches long and an inch wide. Upon these can be written in pencil (so as to be erased later on for reuse) different types of ailments which most closely resemble the symptoms one may have at the moment or think he or she might have. For instance, if a woman experiences a continual lack of energy and her own doctors have failed to diagnose her condition to her satisfaction, she can resort to the use of lots to have God help her pinpoint what her problem may be.

Upon several small pieces of wood, she might then inscribe such maladies as "chronic fatigue syndrome," "mononucleosis," "herpes simplex II," "adrenal insufficiency," "hypoglycemia," "sleep exhaustion" (or insomnia), and "lack of iron." These objects would then be placed into a covered receptacle of some type and vigorously shaken. But not before the woman had knelt by her couch, chair, or bedside and petitioned God in words to this effect:

"Oh God of Heaven and earth. Thou knowest the needs of thy handmaiden here. Thou knowest that thy daughter hast consulted many different specialists, who have been unable to properly diagnose my condition thus far. And as it was with the woman of bloody issue, mentioned by the Apostle Luke, who had squandered her wealth in search of a medical explanation for her peculiar condition, so have I, thy daughter, exhausted reasonable time and efforts and funds in order to find a simple solution to this my pressing problem of a lack of energy, by which I might serve Thee more faithfully.

"Now O God, I ask thee in faith and humility, to bless and consecrate these pieces of wood upon which I have written various likely ailments which most closely correspond to what I may have. I, therefore, ask Thee, O God, in the Name of Thy Only Begotten Son, Jesus Christ, to so ordain that when I pour these bits of wood out in front of me, the one which most nearly fits my particular condition, may fall the closest to me. And by this, I might obtain a clearer understanding than the doctors consulted thus far, were able to provide me with.

"And now I ask Thee for these things in the Name of Thy Son, Jesus Christ, Amen."

Then, while still in a kneeling position, she would shake the covered receptacle well (a large Tupperware mixing bowl with a snap-on lid is adequate) and then, uncovering it, pour out the wooden pieces from a height of about a foot or more upon the floor in front of her. It's best to do this on linoleum or tile rather than a carpet or rug to permit the pieces to bounce more generously once they strike the surface. Also, while pouring out these bits of inscribed wood, the individual should hold the vessel at arm's length from the body while still in a kneeling position, so that the appropriate piece(s) might have sufficient space between where they first make contact with the floor and one's own knees to bounce freely without striking against the person, thereby possibly voiding the legitimacy of the procedure.

In some instances, a repeat of this ritual may be necessary, especially if several bits of wood fall near-to the kneeling person. On the other hand, it could signify two or more likely considerations for the undisclosed malady. In the case of one woman who followed this procedure, the pair of inscribed wood pieces which fell nearest to her bent knees read "hypoglycemia" and "lack of iron." This knowledge directed her to consult books on low blood sugar for dietary advice and to start taking a good iron supplement purchased from her local health food store. In a short time, her persistent fatigue was sufficiently remedied that she could carry out her daily tasks and assignments in a capable and enthusiastic manner.

In a case of something more complex like "chronic fatigue syndrome," had that inscribed wood lot fallen closest to the subject used in this illustration, she might have had to resort to several additional things. One would be to read up on the condition in reliable self-help health books. A second would be to obtain a list of those things, from such references, which would be most likely to help remedy the condition.

Once such a list had been compiled, then the individual would proceed to write each of them on a particular small piece of wood and put them in the covered receptacle. A prayer similar to the one previously mentioned would next be offered, followed by a shaking and dropping of the wooden lots onto the floor while the subject was in a kneeling position. Those several lots falling closest to her knees, would then be the most likely items to take or do in order to correct such "chronic fatigue syndrome."

Finally, after obtaining the desired information from the casting of lots, the subject should remain kneeling and offer up a brief prayer of gratitude unto the Most High God Himself for His kind and merciful influence in the way particular wooden lots may have fallen. All of this ought to be done in the strictest soberness of mind and sincerity of heart, with no malice or discontent or doubt towards anyone or anything harbored at the time such transactions are done. Again, it should be said that such a method ought to be followed only when the person in need is unable to secure sufficient faith for personal revelation or inspiration channeled through the medium of the Holy Ghost into the person's mind or heart.

It might also be imperative to note that the casting of lots for personal health needs is best recommended for simpler rather than complicated maladies. True, it can be judiciously employed to some degree of usefulness in cases like cancer or heart disease. But we get into very serious problems fraught with considerable complications. And wisdom dictates that other means be pursued, besides the casting of lots, for information on how to cope with such complex problems as these. Obviously, the consulting of several different medical and alternative health care specialists would be one of these. Another would be a simple series of tests to determine the progress of said disease. A third would be the personal reading of self-help health books which specifically deal with such topics. Then and only then, should come the casting of lots through faith and hope and prayer in order to obtain higher light and knowledge which man's own resources may have failed to adequately supply.

The procedures outlined are relatively free from the usual hocus-pocus that typically accompanies such purposeful rituals. If honestly used for righteous means, the casting of lots can be of considerable benefit to those of us who for one reason or another, just cannot quite pull down sufficient revelation at the time to endow them with the knowledge they need for this or that malady.

Other Forms of Health Divining:
Astrology and Familiar Spirits

A few words ought to be said about several other forms of ancient divining not mentioned thus far. One of these is the well-known pseudoscience of astrology, but with a somewhat different twist than the present cheap imitations offer. The royal art of astrology is the method of divination for which Old Babylon was famed. Study of the rise of astrology in various Mesopotamian civilizations is still going on a century-and-a-half after the first clay tablets were unearthed in central Iraq. This pertinent evidence which has been remarkably well preserved for such a lengthy period of time (three or four millenniums, at least) is of a rather primitive but useful type. Such astrological omens come chiefly from ancient texts found at the periphery of Mesopotamian influence—in Boghazkeui, Qatna, Mari, and Elam. They testify to the existence of an astrological tradition already diversified at the crucial Old Babylonian period. This is borne out by references, in a later test, to observations of the planet Venus made at the time of the Old Babylonian king Ammisaduqa. The fact that astrological texts were imported to Susa and Hattusa and translated into Elamite and Hittite emphasizes the readiness with which this type of divination was accepted outside Babylonia, even before the rise of astrology.

The bulk of astrological omen texts comes from the library of Assurbanipal. Some were written in Assur and Calah, and others were found in the south, the latter dating mainly from the later period and coming from Babylon, Borsippa, Uruk, Kish, and Nippur. A Middle Babylonian fragment found in Nippur and another found in Nuzi indicate the continuity of the tradition. The "canonical" series, consisting of at least 70 tablets, apart from excerpt texts and tablets with commentaries, is called Enuma Anu Enlil "When Anu and Enlil," after the first words of its solemn bilingual introit. The moon is treated in 23 tablets, then the sun, meteorological phenomena, the planets, and the fixed stars. The time and other circumstances of the disappearance of the old moon, its reappearance, its relation to the sun, and other data on eclipses, offer the "signs" which the series describes and interprets in detail. Less extensive treatment is given halos, strange cloud formations, and the movements of the planets (mainly the planet Venus) among the fixed stars. Meteorological phenomena—thunder, rain, hail, earthquakes—are believed to have ominous validity in matters of state and in predicting peace and war, harvest, and flood. In the archives of Nineveh have been preserved hundreds of reports of astrologers sent to the Assyrian kings in answer to queries occasioned by such phenomena.

A different level of astrology is revealed in texts that date from the fifth (410) and third centuries B.C. These are horoscopes which mention the date of birth, the date of conception, followed by an astronomical report, concluding with predictions of the future of the child. The important thing to remember here about these texts is that their dates prove this type of inferior astrology to be a later development in Babylon. These horoscopes had to be connected with a Selecuid tablet which related the future of a child to certain astronomical conditions, the rising and the movements of planets, eclipses, and other phenomena that occurred at his or her birth.

This is the kind of lesser astrology which is so much in vogue today, but in Old Babylon would have been cast aside as nothing to place much faith or hope in.

How ironic it is these days, in an era of ultramodern space technology and superb scientific achievements with regard to studying the heavens, that no one is able to discern correctly cosmic or meteorological disturbances in relation to human events. For all of our space probes and billion-dollar, orbiting telescopes, we still haven't been able to connect what's happening out there with what will soon be transpiring here on earth.

Consider these things if you will. The births of the Lord Jesus Christ, Moses the great Hebrew Lawgiver, and Abram the "Father of the Faithful," were all attended or preceded by wonderful astronomical events, usually in the form of a sudden appearance of remarkable stars somewhere. In December 1603, the German astronomer Johannes Kepler observed a conjunction of Jupiter and Saturn, joined in March 1604 by Mars. He calculated that these planets were also in conjunction at the time of the Savior's birth in Bethlehem, and could possibly have been the famed Magi's "star" which they followed to Bethlehem. Interestingly, this heavenly phenomenon took place some time in the Spring with Kepler and Jesus, which strongly suggests that His birth in the manger, as carefully detailed in the entire second chapter of Matthew, may have occurred then and not towards the end of December, as the world continues to foolishly believe is the case. (See an excellent treatise on Kepler's theory for this happening in the spring rather than in December in John D. Davis' *Davis Dictionary of the Bible* (4th Ed.), pp. 784-85). Early Mormon Apostle and noted astronomer, Orson Pratt equivocally stated that "the 11th day of April, would be the anniversary of the very day on which Jesus was born; and the 6th day of April the very day on which he was crucified precisely eighteen hundred years prior to the organization of this [the Mormon] Church." (See the Mormon Church publication, the *Journal of Discourses* 13:127, published in Liverpool, England in 1871 for an expansion of his novel and rather theologically sound idea).

Although the *Bible* is silent on the astronomical events surrounding the births of Moses and Abraham, apocryphal and ancient historical sources are not. The "Book of Jasher" (67:4) speaks of a glory attending Moses' birth in these few words: "She brought forth a son, and the whole house was filled with great light as of the light of the sun and moon at the time of their shining." Also near that time as well, the earth moved much closer to the sun for a brief period, producing such intense and "terrible heat in the land of Egypt, which burned up the flesh of man like the sun in his circuit, and it greatly oppressed the Egyptians; and [they] went down to bathe in the river, on account of the consuming heat which burned up their flesh" (Jasher 67:15-16). Likewise did the great Jewish historian, Flavius Josephus, mention great celestial events taking place in the cosmos at the time of Moses' birth (see his *Antiquities of the Jews*, Book II, Chapter 9).

But the most remarkable account of all to show just how well Old

Babylonian omen prognosticating worked may be evidenced in the birth of Abram to Terah's wife at the time that the wicked King Nimrod solidly ruled Mesopotamia with an iron fist. The "Book of Jasher" beautifully lays this marvelous account before us in the first 12 verses of the eighth chapter in this manner:

"And it was in the night that Abram was born, that all the servants of Terah, and all the wise men of Nimrod, and his conjurors came and ate and drank in the house of Terah, and they rejoiced with him on that night.

"And when all the wise men and conjurors went out from the house of Terah, they lifted up their eyes toward heaven that night to look at the stars, and they saw, and behold one very large star came from the east and ran in the heavens, and he swallowed up the four stars from the four sides of the heavens.

"And all the wise men of the king and his conjurors were astonished at the sight, and the sages understood this matter, and they knew of its import.

"And they said to each other, This only betokens the child that has been born to Terah this night, who will grow up and be fruitful, and multiply, and possess all the earth, he and his children forever, and he and his seed will slay great kings, and inherit their lands.

"And the wise men and conjurors went home that night, and in the morning all these wise men and conjurors rose up early, and assembled in an appointed house.

"And they spoke and said to each other, Behold the sight that we saw last night is hidden from the king, it has not been made known to him.

"And should this thing get known to the king in the latter days, he will say to us, why have you concealed this matter from me, and then we shall all suffer death; therefore, now let us go and tell the king the sight which we saw, and the interpretation thereof, and we shall then remain clear.

"That this thing applies to the child that is born to Terah, who will grow up and multiply greatly, and become powerful, and kill all the kings of the earth, and inherit all their lands, he and his seed forever."

It is said on good authority that the births of great men (and women) of history, like Joseph Smith, Jr., the American Prophet, Albert Einstein, the great mathematician, and Gandhi, the great peacemaker, were all attended by minor or major celestial events discernible with the naked eye or a primitive telescope.

In A. H. Charles' *Apocrypha and Pseudepigrapha of The Old Testament* (2:805), brief reference is made in Fragments of a Zadokite Work to the watchers of heaven. In ancient times, these were men of skill and wisdom who held a particular position in the legitimate higher priesthood of God, who continually discerned changes in the cosmos and then were able, by true revelation, to apply such events correctly to mankind in general or specifically. Such an office became lost in time, however, and hasn't as yet been fully restored to the true priesthood on earth today, but in time it will be.

Consider, though, what might have happened if we still had such individuals on earth as they did in ancient Babylon. They would be able to correctly interpret recent cosmic disturbances with similar events now occurring on earth. A case in point would be the recent Mideast War in the Persian Gulf between Iraq (formerly ancient Mesopotamia) and the United States.

Just a week or so before Saddam Hussein invaded tiny neighboring Kuwait, there occurred in our immediate solar system a storm of gigantic proportions that raged across much of the planet Saturn. This unusual storm composed chiefly of ammonia ice crystals was first spotted last summer (1990) by amateur astronomers, prompting excited scientists to convince NASA to allow them to use the Hubble Space Telescope to photograph the area in detail. "It turned out it became something very special," said James Westphal of the California Institute of Technology in Pasadena at a news conference at NASA headquarters where the images were released.

The storm, which was about 150 miles above Saturn's normal upper atmosphere, was about triple the diameter of earth when it was first detected on the ringed planet's equator in mid-1990. The new images showed the storm was then spreading eastward at about 1,000 mph and had stretched nearly completely around the planet's equator to a size of about 200,000 miles—or approximately ten times the size of earth, astrophysical scientists noted.

The size of the storm made it the "largest atmospheric structure currently in the solar system outside the sun," Andrew Ingersoll, a professor of planetary science at Caltech said. Ingersoll said he was uncertain how or why the storm formed. The last time anything like this was spotted on Saturn was in 1929, the same year the stock market crashed and sent this nation into a deep economic depression.

Because it's summer in that part of Saturn, Ingersoll thought that heat from the sun may have helped to trigger the storm's formation from hydrogen and helium gas and liquid from the deep primordial interior of the planet. Scientists continued to study the data fed back to them about this storm from the Hubble Telescope in hopes of learning more about the planet itself, which apparently seems to be more turbulent than was previously imagined.

The point here, of course, is that such unlikely cosmic manifestations have often been connected to or coincided with equally disturbing events here on earth. The ancient Babylonian "watchers" would surely have drawn similarities between the two, but in our own time we have become so sophisticated and led away by our own technological greatness that we have lost the simple ability to connect great heavenly events with things occurring or about to happen here on earth.

This is the true astrology that Old Babylon believed in and practiced frequently, not the garbage touted today in many newspapers and magazines and by phony astrologers. The Savior and Redeemer of the World often referred to such omens Himself, especially when He described His Second Coming, as Matthew 24:29-30 relates:

"Immediately after the tribulation of those days shall the sun be darkened, and the moon shall not give her light, and the stars shall fall from heaven, and the powers of the heavens shall be shaken; and then shall appear the sign of the Son of man in heaven: and then shall all the tribes of the earth mourn, and they shall see the Son of man coming in the clouds of heaven with power and great glory."

No wonder Jesus advised his disciples and the rest of us in our day to always "take heed, watch, and pray" (Mark 13:33) or "watch ye therefore and prays always" (Luke 21:36). By "watching" He surely didn't mean scanning our horoscopes printed in the daily papers, but rather to watch the television or printed news events concerning any unusual astronomical manifestations; and then to pray about such things until correctly informed with genuine information as to how they're connected with events here on earth.

The stars were believed by ancient civilizations to portend coming events. Therefore, they were observed with a view towards prognostication. For even the Old Testament prophet Isaiah (47:13) declared:

"Thou art wearied in the multitude of thy counsels. Let now the astrologers, the stargazers, the monthly prognosticators, stand up, and save thee from these things that shall come upon thee."

Getting to be good at such omen divining as they did in Old Babylon, doesn't require a lot of skill or even too much intelligence. All one has to do is keep abreast of the latest news concerning events in the cosmos and corresponding developments of a different kind here on earth. Then with simple childlike faith and humility, kneel before Almighty God and ask Him about their combined significance. Nothing could be easier than that, and surely it is a lot less expensive and more accurate than consulting conventional astrologers.

The New Testament informs us of several stars to be on the lookout for in the months and years to come. One of these is the "daystar" referred to by Peter (II Peter 1:19), which would rise with the sun in the morning at sometime. Another is the "morning star" mentioned by John the Beloved (Revelation 2:28). A third, particularly nasty and ominous star called "wormwood" of all things, will someday soon "fall from heaven, burning as it were a lamp, and [pollute] the third part of the rivers, and upon the fountains of waters...and many men died of the waters, because they were made bitter" (Revelation 8:10-11). Therefore, it behooves one and all to "watch and pray always" as Christ so wisely recommended be done in our time.

By doing so we obtain peace of mind within ourselves. We aren't frantically driven about by every false rumor or ill report that might otherwise cast fear into our hearts. By having this inward calmness of soul, we can enjoy good, sound mental and emotional health, while everyone around us is going plumb crazy from the inner agitation such cosmic cataclysms are bound to produce.

Turning now to another form of health divining, we discover that of consulting with familiar spirits. In ancient times, the spirit of a deceased individual could be summoned up by the right kind of mediums in order to hold special consultations (Deuteronomy 18:11). Sometimes such familiar spirits appeared to speak from the earth (Isaiah 29:4), or at other times, to dwell in the controlling medium itself (Leviticus 20:27). The former way, of the spirit rising up and speaking from the earth, was believed to be more of God, whereas the latter example of such a spirit entering someone else's body and channeling its thoughts through that person's mind by way of temporary possession, was believed to be of the devil.

The medium was called the possessor or lord of a spirit (1 Samuel 28:7). It revealed the future as a rule (Isaiah 8:19). It was either a special spirit which was believed to always respond to the summons of the medium, as the English rendering would lead one to suppose, and who might raise other ghosts. Or it was any spirit whom the medium desired to call forth from the "other world." Hence, I Samuel 28:8 which involved the woman known as the "Witch of Endor," is capable of either interpretation. "Divine by the ghost" in you or "whom I shall name."

Now to have consulted with familiar spirits in ancient Israel was considered to be rank apostasy from Jehovah (Leviticus 19:31; Isaiah 8:19). Under the Mosaic law, persons pretending to possess such power of consulting with familiar spirits were put to death (Leviticus 19:31;20:6,27; Deuteronomy 17:11). Saul carried out this enactment, but when sorely troubled about his fate, he sought out a woman of Endor who had this gift or ability, asking her to bring back his former friend Samuel from the Spirit World. She succeeded in doing this for him, but became sorely afraid once she learned who Saul's true identity was. However, he comforted her not to worry about losing her life for doing what he had asked of her.

Not all those who consulted with familiar spirits in ancient times were considered to be of the devil or working by the powers of the evil one. In the case of the good woman from Endor, we have a fine example of a noble-hearted soul who employed her spiritual abilities and talents in the pursuit of helping others, as in the instance of Saul. She had lived a righteous enough life to have earned the power from God to call up the righteous departed such as Samuel and his family, and not some demons impersonating them. The *Bible* clearly informs us that King Saul recognized Samuel upon seeing him and knew exactly who it was!

Therefore, if one lives his or her life circumspectly, by the light and truth in his or her possession, and endeavors to walk always in childlike humility, faith, love, and prayer before God, then there is no reason why such an individual cannot call upon a dearly departed loved one or friend in times of need. Such a thing ought to be done properly in a prayer to God first, and then within the context of that same prayer to God, petition a favorite loved one or trusted friend to render advice from the Spirit World, *when all other reasonable methods have failed.*

From the Babylonians and ancient scriptures we can learn so much about true divining that may help us with personal mental, emotional, and physical health problems of every description. Caution and common sense obviously have to be used when attempting such a thing for righteous purposes, lest the devil and his minions enter in and create considerable mischief in the process. This is why ordinary faith and prayer and personal revelation are the safest mediums by which to obtain Higher knowledge about yourself. But, in the event these may not work as well as we would like them to, it's nice to know we have things like the casting of lots, omen prognosticating, consulting familiar spirits and, most of all, prayer itself to resort to in times of pressing need.

CHAPTER FOUR

WHAT THE HEBREWS CONTRIBUTED FOR STAYING WELL

Manna, the Food of Life

Manna, the name appointed by the ancient Israelites to the miraculous life-giving food provided to them by God during their desert sojourns for nearly four decades, has remained as inscrutable as several other things have in the Near and Far East. Even to this day, it continues to baffle the likes of great Biblical scholars and archaeologists as to its true identity.

Well did the Hebrews ask one another when they first saw it lying there upon the ground: "What is it? for they knew not what it was" (Exodus 16:15). A pastor friend of mine in a small town in Texas was asked by one of his inquisitive teenage parishioners during a typical Sunday School *Bible* class that I just happened to be attending then, "Reverend, can you explain to us exactly what this manna stuff was made of?" To which, the minister jokingly replied, "Would you settle for an explanation of the resurrection instead?" This is how baffling the matter of manna has become in the minds of theologians and scientists alike; for who of them has yet correctly identified its true nature?

In lieu of the facts, a myriad of hypotheses have sprung up over the years in various attempts to satisfactorily explain this stuff. One of the more novel approaches has been to define manna as a natural product already in existence then, as opposed to a first-time created substance in the wilderness.

Many scientists hoping to neatly skirt the issue of this compelling problem, have offered what they imagine to be an obvious explanation for manna. Throughout the Sinai Peninsula, certain insects are known to produce honeydew excretions on tamarisk twigs during the month of June. In the evening, these drops fall from the trees to the ground, where they remain until the heat of the hot desert sun brings forth the ants to remove them. Such drops are small, sticky, light-colored, and sugary-sweet, thereby fitting some but not all of the Biblical descriptions mentioned in Exodus 16 and Numbers 11.

But, according to *Davis' Dictionary of the Bible* (4th Ed.) such an explanation must be rejected for several reasons. First, the substance is extremely purgative if consumed in great quantities;

therefore, only minimal use can be obtained from it as a source of nourishment. Secondly, even in the best years of abundant production, there just isn't enough yield in the entire peninsula to feed the bedouins who utilize it, let alone hope to feed half-a-million wandering Israelites on a daily basis. It seems that we have to look elsewhere for an alternative solution.

Almost 70 years ago, Dr. Paul Haupt, an instructor in Semitic languages at Johns Hopkins University, proposed what some have since considered to be a more logical explanation as to what manna may have been. He proclaimed that the Israelites, under the capable leadership of Moses, ate nutritive lichen similar in content to Iceland moss and the reindeer moss, which, in times of great drought and famine, have served as reliable food sources for large numbers of people in the arid steppes of various countries stretching from Algeria to Mongolia. These edible lichens, he reported in the August 1922, *American Journal of Pharmacy*, contained not only starchy substances, but sometimes a small amount of saccharine matter. After gathering these mosses each day, the Israelites would then grind them up in their stone mortars and mix the resulting powder with some of the honey-like drops from the punctured bark of tamarisk trees.

His explanation, while by no means the definitive word on the subject, at least brings us closer to understanding this mystery better than just about anything else has. However, beyond Haupt's own opinion is still another more viable proposal.

An entirely new concept proposed here is that manna more closely resembled a singe-celled, fresh-water alga called chlorella than anything else considered so far. A common mistake made by many has been to compare the color and taste ascribed to manna—"it was like coriander seed, white; and the taste of it was like wafers made with honey" (Exodus 16:31)—with known substances in the region like tamarisk drops, for instance.

But I propose looking at some of the other, often-neglected properties of manna, which compare favorably with chlorella. Exodus 16:13 clearly associates early morning dew with the development of manna. In a little tract on chlorella by Drs. W.H. Lee and M. Rosenbaum, fresh, sweet water is necessary for the multiplication of this unique alga. When the dew had evaporated, there lay a small round thing upon the ground. There are two points to remember here about chlorella: (A) It is microscopically small but reproduces at an incredible rate, and (B) it needs plenty of sunlight to proliferate so quickly. The dividing and subdividing of just a single cell in 63 days could generate enough chlorella to equal the volume of this entire planet, believe it or not!

As an anthropologist who has made a lifetime study of the *Bible* and its different types of people, I have come to recognize another thing with regard to manna which has been overlooked by nearly all scholars until now. This is in the area of nutrition. The next to last verse of Exodus 16 explains that "the children of Israel did eat manna forty years," which can be interpreted as meaning that it was probably the chief source of nourishment for them during this entire period of time. Thus, manna was about the most complete food they had available at the time.

Some of the nutritional aspects of chlorella qualify it as the possible manna which the Children of Israel might have consumed for over four decades. For one thing, it's nearly 60% protein, compared with just 39% for soybeans, 10% for wheat, and a measly 7% for rice. It has eight essential amino acids, which comprise the principle components of pure protein. Chlorella protein, in fact, compares favorably with beef, lamb, pork, fish, or chicken, save for the amino acid methionine, which is lower in chlorella than in meat.

Nutrient-wise, chlorella contains respectable amounts of vitamin C, provitamin A (betacarotene), most of the B-complex group, and vitamins E and K. Rich in minerals and trace elements, chlorella yields generous amounts of calcium, phosphorus, potassium, iron, iodine, and others which are necessary for maintaining muscle energy and constitutional stamina.

In addition to the 60% protein content, chlorella also consists of about 20% carbohydrates and fats. These nutrients provide the body with a great deal of strength and help it endure through particularly difficult physical ordeals similar to what the ancient Israelites must have experienced during their long desert sojourn.

Chlorella has been widely studied throughout the earth. Japan, America, France, Israel, India, the Soviet Union, Bulgaria, and Czechoslovakia have all participated in extensive research with this most remarkable alga. From the accumulated scientific material published thus far, one is led to wonder whether or not chlorella was specifically created with the human race in mind. And though its actual origins will undoubtedly remain obscure, due to its biological resemblance to the human cell, we must ask ourselves, "Can chlorella, indeed, be the ancient manna which God gave for sustenance to the Hebrews?" No other single source of nutrition could have so thoroughly sustained the Children of Israel for 40 years as this manna-like substance called chlorella.

This alga's ability to multiply rapidly, certainly could have fed the hungry masses Moses was leading to the Promised Land. Also, chlorella's remarkable ability to boost the body's own immune defenses seems to have kept the Hebrews pretty healthy and disease-free.

A study published in Japanese in the *Journal of The Kanazawa Medical University* (Supplement 10:205-10, 1985) demonstrated that chlorella significantly increased the number of macrophages (scavenger immune cells) in tumor-bearing mice, thereby producing an anti-tumor effect and prolonging the lives of these rodents. Other recent work appearing in *Cancer Immunology and Immunotherapy* (19:73-78, 1985) has shown that another form of white blood cell, called the polymorphonuclear leukocyte, is activated by chlorella extract in a nonspecific way to fight cancer cells. Thus, chlorella can be useful in both the prevention and treatment of cancer, when used in conjunction with a prudent diet and other acceptable forms of nutritive therapy.

Chlorella's antiviral capacity is also good against milder infections. Dr. Shirota Minoru and his team were the first to isolate these strong antiviral components from the lipid fractions of chlorella. They were found to be very effective against viruses belonging to the entero and adeno groups in vitro. The same strong antiviral activities have also been described by others in *Applied Microbiology* (16:1809-10, 1968).

In this last cited study, chlorella was tested extensively on enlisted sailors in the Japanese navy. This was done in 1966, while some of them were sailing from Tokyo to New Zealand during a 95-day period. The control group consisted of 513 crewmen and the experimental group consisted of 458 crewmen all between the ages of 19 and 30 who took two grams of chlorella tablets daily. Six times during the voyage, the men were checked for colds and the results tabulated. At the end of the trip, those sailors taking chlorella tablets regularly had 571 colds, while the control group had nearly a thousand colds. Thus, 26.5% less colds occurred in those taking two grams of chlorella daily.

Hideo Nakayama, age 77, is chairman of the Japan Chlorella Research Center and Medicinal Plant Institute on the island of Hokkaido. He is also one of the earliest proponents of the many wonderful health virtues contained in this green "manna." In responding to a reporter's question about, "What is the ingredient of chlorella that has such a powerful effect in overcoming sickness?" he responded this way, "Scientific analyses have succeeded in separating out a large number of important constituents, all of which comprise a single chlorella cell. Yet no individual ingredient is specifically responsible for this. It is the unique combination of *all* the vitamins, minerals, amino acids, and enzymes present that makes this alga work so well in the human body."

In a time when the world is becoming increasingly polluted, it's comforting to know that there's something like chlorella around which can be easily taken and yet do the system so much good. This life-giving food that appears to have also been the ancient desert manna of the Israelites (or at least its near-equivalent), can be obtained from most health food stores or nutrition centers under the brand-name of Sun Chlorella. If not available in your immediate area, just call or write YSK American Corp., 4025 Spencer St., Torrance, CA. 90503 (1-800-537-0077) for further information on how to obtain some of this "miracle food" for yourself!

The Dietary Laws of Moses

Awhile back, I sat down to a delicious Sunday dinner at the home of a dear friend of mine in Pueblo, Colorado, who happens to be minister of a small evangelical church in the area. Everything on the table seemed pretty good from a health perspective until his wife brought out the main course from the kitchen—a lovely baked ham. When my eyes caught this, I groaned within. To which my friend, who must have heard this muffled complaint, asked, "I hope you're not allergic to pork?" 1 shook my head in the negative.

Whereupon, he laughed good-naturedly and inquired: I presume you're still Christian? 1 mean, you haven't gone off and changed your religion suddenly and become Jewish or New Age vegetarian or something like that, I hope?" "No," I wearily said. "It's just that Leviticus 11-7-8 warns us against eating pork in any form: "And the swine...he is unclean to you; of [its] flesh shall ye not eat, and [its] carcass shall ye not touch; [for it is] unclean to you."

"Oh, come on, lighten up good buddy," he chirped, while slapping my back at the same time. "Those laws were meant for the Hebrew people but not us," he finished.

His opinion pretty much sums up the attitude of nearly all Christians today—those dietary laws given by Moses were for Old Testament times and those of the Jewish faith, but not for anyone else. Yet, they completely miss the point of the *Bible* altogether when they explain them away in this haphazard manner. As the Reverend Billy Graham said some years ago in one of his many famous evangelical crusades: "You either take the *Bible* as containing the full Word of God or you don't take it at all!" According to him, there can be no (what he called) "partitioning" of God's Word into what we might accept and into what should be discarded because it's either "old-fashioned, outdated or just doesn't make sense." The dietary regulations handed down by Moses seem to fall into this last category for millions of devout Christians. But their thinking in this respect couldn't be more wrong!

Those not acquainted with Jewish culture sometimes imagine that kosher food laws are some kind of health laws, but this isn't correct. Though many of them do make sense from a health perspective, especially historically, yet that has never been their true justification. In fact, one of the most meaningful explanations of the dietary laws of Moses is the ethical approach, which I. Grunfeld summarized very nicely in his book, *The Jewish Dietary Laws* (London, 1927):

"And ye shall be men of a holy calling unto Me, and ye shall not eat any meat that is torn in the field" (Exodus 22:30). Holiness or self-sanctification is a moral term; it is identical with...moral freedom or moral autonomy. Its aim is the complete self-mastery of man.

To the superficial observer it seems that men who do not obey the law are freer than law-abiding men because they can follow their own inclinations. In reality, however, such men are subject to the most cruel bondage; they are slaves of their own instincts, impulses, and desires. The first step towards emancipation from the tyranny of animal inclinations in man is, therefore, a voluntary submission to the moral law. The constraint of law is the beginning of human freedom... Thus the fundamental idea of Jewish ethics, holiness, inseparably connected with the idea of Law; and the dietary laws occupy a central position in that system of moral discipline which is the basis of all Jewish laws.

The three strongest natural instincts in man are the impulses of food, sex, and acquisition. Judaism does not aim at the destruction of these impulses, but at their control and indeed their santification. It is the law which spiritualizes these instincts and transfigures them into legitimate joys of life.

While Grunfeld's excellent explanation of the exact purposes for these particular laws may apply more directly to Jews themselves, yet they also have some carry over to the lives of Bible-believing Christians as well. Even Ellen G. White, founder of the Seventh-Day Adventist religion, a Christian sect well known for its strict dietary regimen, had the good sense to realize that foods like pork were never designed by God to be eaten. Furthermore, she noted in her *Counsels on Diet and Foods* (Washington, D.C., 1938):

Eating, drinking and dressing all have a direct bearing upon our spiritual advancement. Intemperance in eating and in drinking and the indulgence of base passions, have benumbed the fine sensibilities, so that sacred things have been placed upon a level with common things.

Thus, what Grunfeld, White, and others have had to say about the dietary laws of Moses is this: Adhering to them as much as possible is a dramatic step towards achieving greater holiness of body, mind, and soul, for these laws tend to "spiritualize and transfigure" our baser compulsive instincts such as hunger into higher, more nobler and joyful feelings.

This then ought to be the reason why Christians everywhere would want to follow Moses' laws about diet more strictly than what they presently do. While excluding pork from your diet may not necessarily make you a saint overnight, it will certainly please God enough to endow you with a greater outpouring of His Holy Spirit. And the more dietary sacrifices you make for Him, the closer you will be drawn into His Presence or, that is, the more like Him you will eventually become!

The kosher laws themselves are many and varied. But for our purposes here we intend to focus just on those having to do with combining milk and meat and the proper selection of suitable animal flesh. The first law appears in Exodus 23:19: "Thou shalt not seethe a kid in its mother's milk." This injunction is repeated a total of three different times in the *Pentateuch* or *Five Books of Moses.* Kosher laws demand that a total separation of meat and milk must always be maintained throughout the meal preparation, thus necessitating two sets of dishes, cookware, and eating utensils, each to be used with the appropriate "dairy" or "meat" food.

I recall a rather unintentional but somewhat humorous incident in this regard when I stayed overnight with a devout Jewish friend of mine and his wife, Mr. and Mrs. Joel Bree, of Brooklyn, New York sometime in the Spring of 1986. I had driven back to New York City to speak at a large health convention and appear on a local network TV talk show.

Joel invited a colleague of mine (who had traveled with me) and me to his home, where we had dinner and stayed the night. The next morning his wife told us to go ahead and help ourselves to some food in their kitchen, while she was dressing one of their younger children. We were looking for some plates and eating utensils for our fried eggs, toast, and slices of cold roast beef. In opening different cupboard doors, we discovered the items we had been looking for and put our food on them. When she came back into the kitchen awhile later and saw what we were using, she inquired which cupboard we had obtained them from.

We dutifully pointed to the one they came from. Whereupon, she gave us a rather exasperated look, but said nothing. Upon inquiry, however, she was kind enough to point out that we had used plates, knives, and forks intended solely for meat and nothing else. She then went to another cupboard, opened it, and pointing to the utensils there, said, "These are for our dairy products, like eggs, milk, and cheese." I asked just what would have to be done to "restore" the plates and utensils we had mistakenly used to their proper kosher status. She heaved a sigh and said, "Oh, we'll have to call in our Rabbi and have him go through a lengthy process to sanctify them all over again, but don't worry about it."

This aspect of the Mosaic dietary law needn't apply to Christian households, however. The other part should, in that dairy and meat foods must be eaten separately. Which means the complete elimination of such foods as cheeseburgers and the use of dairy (coffee) creamers at meat meals. Also, the usual custom for most "Kosher Jews" to wait at least four or six hours after a meat meal before having a dairy food, ought to apply to Christians as well.

This makes good health sense from a medical point of view. The fats which comprise dairy foods and different meats vary in their molecular and chemical makeups. And they are digested differently. I'll spare the reader complex scientific jargon to fully explain it and simply say that the liver handles each type of fat (dairy and meat) differently!

A lady in Houston, Texas once asked me, after I had finished a sermon on "The Diet of Daniel" at the All-Black Grace Congregational Church, what she could do about getting rid of migraine headaches she suffered from periodically. After a little inquiry into her eating habits, I felt impressed to tell her to cut down on both her milk and cheese and meat intakes and to consume them at different mealtimes! I remember that she looked at me kind of funny at first, but I reminded her that she had sought for my advice and should follow it, no matter how odd it may have seemed at the time. About a month later, I received a scribbled note from her to the effect that "my migraines are gone, and I thank the Lord and you for having done it." This was obviously a bit overstated, since I'm just a mortal and because the inspiration had come from God; but, nonetheless, it worked for her!

The other part of Moses' dietary laws has to do with the right selection of meats best suited for the human body. Verses 1 through 8 of Leviticus 11 remind us that only those mammals which both chew their cud and are cloven (or split) hoofed are acceptable in the sight of God. I should note here that these particular animals are all herbivores or plant-eating ungulates. Consequently, beef, lamb, mutton, deer, and so forth are all right, but rabbit and pork (bacon, ham, and sausage) are verboten! And this because "their flesh... [is] unclean."

Next in line are verses 13 through 19 which have to do with acceptable fowl that may be eaten. Clearly, as these verses show, birds of prey are totally disqualified. S. H. Dresner and S. Siegel in their own work, *The Jewish Dietary Laws* (New York, 1966) cited the following characteristics of those birds which the dietary laws of Moses permit to be consumed: (1). They must not be birds of prey. (2). They must not have a front toe. (3). They must have a craw (and a double-skin stomach, easily separated). (4). They must be able to catch food thrown into the air, then place it on the ground and tear it with their bills before eating it.

Now, according to Dr. Joe M. Regenstein, an Assistant Professor of Food Sciences in the Departments of Poultry and Food Science at Cornell University, writing in the January, 1979 issue of *Food Technology* on the dietary laws of Moses, turkey is prohibited because it fails to meet these four essential criteria. Along with turkey, chicken should also be excluded from the diet, simply because they have front toes (which are clipped off at birth) and they prey on the other sick chickens, pecking them to death and eating bits and pieces of their carcasses in the process. Other birds, however, like pheasant, quail, goose, and duck are permissible.

However, for most Christians it's probably going to take more proof than Old Testament scriptures and modern Jewish interpretation of them before they become fully convinced to leave both fowls alone! De Lamar Gibbons, M.D., practiced medicine for almost 20 years in Banding, San Juan County, Utah, and on the nearby Navajo Indian Reservation in Monument Valley. After this, he served until just recently as the Director of Medical Research for *The Saturday Evening Post* in Indianapolis.

In the Sunday, November 29th, 1987 edition of *The Salt Lake [Utah] Tribune*, a major article by him entitled, "Indians Hold Key to Cancer," appeared in the "Common Carrier" section of this newspaper. In his opening remarks, he noted that he and several other doctors who had worked among the Navajos for many years had noticed an almost total absence of cancer.

In reviewing their poor diets and lack of adequate cleanliness, he couldn't find anything obvious which might be cancer-preventing. The Navajos as a group eat a high-fat diet consisting of mutton stew, bread deep-fried in mutton tallow, potato chips, soda pop, coffee, beer, candy and Twinkies. They eat virtually no fiber and no vegetables. The nutritional content of their diet is a disaster! Their sanitation is often unbelievably bad. Many draw water from open creeks and have no sanitary facilities (not even out-houses, much less indoor plumbing and running water). In short, they do everything wrong, according to the health authorities. And yet they do not get cancer! They must be doing something right that the rest of us are doing wrong.

Although Navajos suffer from many other diseases, such as hypertension, obesity, diabetes, Bright's disease (a kidney ailment), and coronary problems on account of their high-fat and high-carbohydrate diets, yet they have virtually no cancer! Dr. Gibbons said that between 1960 and 1973 the Monument Valley Hospital where he worked, had 13,000 admissions, 98% being Navajo. Of all the patients doctors screened, a mere 13 had cancer and half of these cases were Caucasians!

Further investigation, however, did turn up two intriguing factors to explain why cancer is nearly absent from our nation's largest Native American tribe. For one thing, Navajos thoroughly cook all meat they consume, usually by boiling it to death. Consequently, this destroys all cancer-producing viruses in the animal flesh they're eating. It also helps to "cook out" many harmful chemical antibiotics and hormones which are known to cause cancer.

But the more important discovery made was that the entire tribe does not eat chicken, eggs, or turkey! Those very few who do, invariably contract cancer at some point in their lives. In the course of the past 30 years, only one of the 5,000 San Juan County [Utah] Navajos has been found to have developed prostate cancer. This cancer becomes almost universal in aged non-Indian men. Equally remarkable was the discovery that this individual was different from the others of his tribe in another way. He broke a sacred taboo. He raised chickens and ate eggs.

Faithful Navajos shun birds. They believe the flight of birds is not accomplished through the application of the physical laws of aerodynamics. To them birds are supported in the air by spooky-magic, and are thus to be avoided. Chickens are carriers of several viruses, such as Marek's and fowl leukosis viruses that cause cancer in the chickens. These viruses are passed into the eggs and millions of non-Navajos eat them. A moment's consideration would tell one that eating even partially cooked eggs would be extremely dangerous. Some of these chicken cancer viruses are also of the same retrovirus family that the AIDS agent belongs to.

Here then we have several hundred thousand people, most of whom still hold to their own Native American religious traditions, who practice at least some important dietary common sense that the rest of us do not. Dr. Gibbons concluded his highly interesting article by saying that these people should be further studied by all of us. They are clearly doing some things right that the majority of us are not doing correctly. It is important for all of us to adopt these two important principles—boiling our meat and avoiding poultry and eggs—into our own lives to reduce our risks of cancer.

The final portion of this chapter reviews what types of seafood are acceptable before the Lord and which ones aren't. Going back to verses 9 through 12 of the 11th chapter of Leviticus, we find several interesting things stressed:

1. Only fish with fins and scales can be safely eaten.

2. This "fins and scales" requirement is repeated three times in just four verses.

3. The word "abominable" which is synonymous with "hateful" or "detestable," never appears with pork, but is used also three

times by God in these four verses to accurately reflect His own particular feelings in regard to all other seafood not measuring up to this "fins and scales" requirement.

According to Regenstein's article on these Mosaic dietary laws in *Food Technology Journal*, all shellfish (molluscan and crustacean) are prohibited.

For those with the "seafood lover" side in many of them, it probably means an arduous and painful experience to deny themselves future pleasures in dining on succulent lobster, shrimp, crab, scallops, oysters, and the like. Still, knowing human nature as well as I do, a good many of the body of Christ will continue to gorge themselves with such seafood "abominations" and keep on ignoring the Divine injunction expressly prohibiting such items from the diet: "Ye shall not eat of their flesh, but...have [it] in abomination!"

If scriptural convincing isn't enough to avoid these awful seafoods, then maybe scientific proof will be. The following list consists of short summaries and excerpts taken from a number of reports about some of the hazardous substances found in prohibited seafoods; this material appeared in a variety of scientific publications published in the last decade or less.

The state of California regularly issues a six-month quarantine on the harvesting of mussels (clams and scallops) because during this period they acquire extremely high concentrations of a deadly toxin very poisonous to humans and animals (*The Lawrence Review of Natural Products*, June 1983). High naturally occurring concentrations of dimethylamine and methylamine have been detected in squid, octopus, and shrimp. Strong epidemiological evidence exists to show that they are implicated in the etiology of gastric cancer (*Food Chemistry and Toxicology* 21:143, 1983).

Shellfish contain gutfuls of germs that could send people to the intensive care unit of their local hospitals within minutes. Organisms that cause cholera, gastroenteritis, hepatitis A, and a host of minor diseases, as well as major toxins, can be seafood-borne, especially by shellfish (*American Health*, April 1985)!

A study was made of 103 outbreaks of gastroenteritis associated with consumption of shellfish. In 22 outbreaks occurring during the summer months, 56% of people who consumed raw clams, and 26% of those who consumed only clams that were steamed, had gastroenteritis. Hepatitis A infection occurred in 5% of people who ate clams in five of the early outbreaks. In 81 winter outbreaks, 92% of people who ate clams had gastrointestinal symptoms, especially nausea and diarrhea. Oysters were implicated in 11 outbreaks. Laboratory studies revealed a major etiological role for Norwalk virus, particularly in the winter outbreaks. Dr. D.L. Morse of the Bureau of Communicable Disease Control with the New York State Department of Health in Albany, suggested that the public *abstain from the consumption of shellfish* as much as possible (*New England Journal of Medicine*, March 13, 1986). Even shellfish that has been government certified clean has been found to contain harmful microorganisms which have caused viral hepatitis in many people who've consumed them (*University of California, Berkeley Wellness Letter*, June 1986).

A large number of outbreaks of crab poisoning have occurred at different times in the past several years on Negros Island in the Philippines among those for whom such crustaceans have been traditional foods for many, many decades. Tetrodotoxin and paralytic shellfish toxins are the isolated poisons known to be responsible for inducing so much sickness among the natives (*Agricultural and Biological Chemistry* 50:593, 1986).

Okadaic acid has been discovered as the causative toxin of a particular nasty disease in man known as diarrhetic shellfish poisoning, which has afflicted thousands of Japanese and European seafood lovers in recent years (*Agricultural and Biological Chemistry* 50:2853, 1986).

The Center for Disease Control (CDC) in Atlanta, Georgia reported an alarming increase of parasite (tapeworm and roundworm) infections due to the popularity of sushi. The newsletter which cited this, expressly warned its readers to "cross that sushi bar off your list!" (*University of California, Berkeley, Wellness Letter*, March 1987).

High levels of particularly nasty bacteria were still detected in freshly shucked oysters just a few hours later, even after they had been thoroughly pasteurized and properly refrigerated (*Journal of Food Science* 53:235, 1988)! Certain crustaceans such as shrimp, lobster, and crab are *extremely high* in cholesterol levels, more so, in fact than other fish or skinless chicken is. Shrimp especially is exceptionally high in cholesterol (*Bon Appetit*, June 1988).

In the Summer of 1988 nearly 100 tourists and residents of Panama City, Florida ate some oysters from one of the prime hogging grounds, Watson Bayou, an oyster-rich bay now contaminated by sewage overflows. All of them soon became strickened with the liver disease hepatitis A (*Wall Street Journal*, Thursday, June 8th, 1989).

From the overwhelming evidence just given, people should think twice from now on before consuming seafood that does not have fins and scales. Even in cultures largely dependent upon such seafood items, these prohibited things should be completely avoided. In May, 1986 I attended an international conference on medicinal plants and acupuncture in the city of Taipei, Taiwan.

About 1,000 delegates in all were there.

Some of us from North America, scientists from the United States and medical doctors from Montreal, Canada, were cordially invited to an evening banquet with the mayor of Taipei. Among the many entree items constantly being brought to our individual tables, was something called cucumber soup. Not being much of a seafood buff myself, I just assumed that it was the garden vegetable bearing the same name.

The waiter at our table ladled up generous servings of this liquid into each of our bowls. I was too busily engaged in conversation with several American pharmacologists to pay much mind to what was then put in front of me. I paused just long enough to bow my head and invoke a quiet blessing upon my food, before continuing the discussion with my other colleagues seated beside me. Before concluding the "Amen" portion of my prayer, however, a still, small voice whispered to my mind, "You shouldn't be eating this because it violates those dietary laws of God you've tried hard to follow all these years."

To say that I was surprised is an understatement. I soon made an inquiry about this cucumber soup, and learned that the sea cucumber isn't really a vegetable at all, but a relative of the starfish and sand dollar. The parts used are its tentacles and slimy guts. Whereupon, I kindly passed on it and waited for our Peking duck to arrive. Needless to say, about 13 of our group came down with diarrhea, abdominal cramps, nausea, and vomiting that night and were pretty sick well into the next day. I was thankful to God for having escaped because of His timely warning that I carefully listened to and obeyed to the letter!

One thing I've discovered in my many years working with herbs and spices, is that ginger root tea makes a wonderful recovery remedy for those afflicted with any type of shellfish poisoning. Simply simmer one heaping tablespoonful of freshly grated ginger root in 1 1/2 pints of boiling water for 5 minutes and then steep it away from stove heat for an additional 25 minutes. Strain and drink one cup warm every couple of hours, or as needed.

The dietary laws of God given to Moses have just as much validity and bearing upon us today as they did anciently upon the Hebrew people. If we apply them more consistently and strictly in our lives, then we will be spared the pain, suffering, and agony which comes to those who deliberately or unintentionally ignore them. For as the Lord Himself declared unto Moses then so too do His same words ring true with us at the close of the 20th century:

This is the law of the beasts, and of the fowl, and of every living creature in the waters... To make a difference between the unclean and the clean, and between the beast that may be eaten and the beast that may not be eaten (Leviticus 11:46-47).

Garlic, the All-Around Supplement

During their several centuries stay in the land of Egypt, the Children of Israel became intimately familiar with garlic and onion, especially the former. They used it so much that one would have thought it was almost a national fad. In truth, though, it was probably the single dietary supplement that kept them healthy as a nation for so long without contracting the many epidemics that occurred in Egypt. So much did they enjoy it, that after leaving Egypt they moaned and groaned for more of it.

From Tuesday to Thursday, August 28-30, 1990, I attended the First World Garlic Congress held at the prestigious and historic Willard Hotel in Washington, D.C., within walking distance of the White House. More than 200 other scientists and health professionals convened to hear the latest scientific and medical evidence about garlic:

Helps prevent cancer. Researchers in mainland China and Italy found it cut people's risk of stomach cancer.

Cuts risk of heart attacks and strokes. Researchers in India say it cut death rates from coronary artery disease.

Reduces serum cholesterol and triglyceride levels. American researchers found it dramatically lowered cholesterol and triglycerides in rats and rabbits.

Hypotensive effect observed. Two Danish pharmacognosists reported a lowering of blood pressure in hypertensive cases using garlic extract regularly.

Hypoglycemic aspect detected. A growing body of evidence indicates garlic may be useful to diabetics. Antifungal properties noticed. Garlic stops Candida albicans.

Odor-modified (kyolic) garlic accomplishes all of the above and more! Doctors hail Japanese garlic extract made by Wakunaga as an amazing dietary supplement for good health.

According to a report delivered by William 1. Blot of the National Cancer Institute in Bethesda, Maryland, garlic and other members of the onion genus *Allium* could erect a barrier against human cancer cells. Blot and his colleges questioned nearly 4,000 people from regions of Italy and mainland China—including areas with some of the highest rates of stomach cancer in the world—about their diets for the past 20 years. Those who recalled eating the most Allium vegetables showed the lowest incidence of stomach cancers by as much as 60%.

Arun Bordia of the Tagore Medical College in Udaipur, India reported tracking 432 heart attack survivors for 3 years, during which time half of the participants consumed the juice from 6-10 cloves of fresh garlic daily. (The average Indian eats 1-2 cloves a day, he said). Many of the others took a garlic scented placebo. Overall, the garlic eaters suffered 32% fewer recurrent heart attacks, and 45% fewer deaths from heart attacks, than the unsupplemented patients did.

Nilofer Qureshi of Advanced Medical Research in Madison, Wisconsin fed aged garlic extract and s-allyl-cysteine (a sulphur component derived from garlic) to 60 chickens. After four weeks of daily garlic supplements at doses as high as 8% of body weight, the garlic-supplemented chickens showed decreases in cholesterol of as much as 30% when compared to six chickens receiving no garlic. "More importantly, low-density lipoproteins (which transport cholesterol to clog-prone heart arteries) decreased by as much as 50%," she stated in her report at the convention. Chickens, she noted, synthesize cholesterol a lot like humans do, which explains why she decided to use them as the animal models to work with.

Two pharmacognosists from the University of Helsinki in Finland, Drs. Jari Kiviranta and Raimo Hiltunen, spoke Wednesday afternoon between 4:40 and 5:05 p.m. They presented a summary of their word with hypertensive rats, which received garlic extract regularly to lower their blood pressures.

Dr. Benjamin Lau, a practicing physician and microbiologist with Loma Linda School of Medicine in Loma Linda, California, spoke on the "Health Benefits of Aged Garlic Extract." He has treated some of his diabetic patients with aged (kyolic) garlic extract and discovered that it helped to lower their blood sugar levels. Interestingly, the kyolic extract *didn't* adversely affect those with hypoglycemia, but raw garlic did; this essentially was his response to a question I put to him during a brief question and answer session at the end of his talk. Dr. Lau has also tested kyolic garlic on various types of cancer cells and discovered their growth was suppressed.

Dr. Lau, one of his associate microbiologists, and a physiologist also tested kyolic garlic for its antifungal activity. Their report, which appeared in the October, 1990 issue of *International Clinical Nutrition Review* was briefly mentioned at the garlic conference. Results showed that kyolic garlic inhibited the growth of Candida albicans or yeast infection.

Many of the scientists there whom I later interviewed, had conducted their experiments using kyolic garlic. They felt that it held greater medical promise than raw garlic did. Some, in fact, believed that the Wakunaga Pharmaceutical Company of Japan, had even made "a better garlic" than the one Nature came up with originally. Kyolic garlic is available throughout the U.S. and Canada in most health food stores and nutrition centers.

In the event you cannot obtain this remarkable garlic extract in your area, write or call:

Wakunaga of America Co., Ltd.
23501 Madero
Mission Viejo, CA. 92691
(1-800)-421-2998 / Calif. (800)—544-5800

CHAPTER FIVE

DIAGNOSES AND HERBAL CURES FROM ANCIENT CHINA

Diagnoses

The following information is broken up into different segments under this major subheading. While an alphabetical arrangement isn't always followed, such as Acupuncture coming before Diagnoses, within particular segments where there may be multiple items listed an alphabetical order is utilized. Most entries are brief and to the point, except in a few instances where additional explanation is necessary.

In Chinese medicine there are four traditional categories by which physicians can examine their respective patients: visual inspection (wangzhen), hearing and smell (wénzhen), questioning the patient directly (wʻenzhen), and touching the patient's body (qiezhen). By means of these four, different parts of the body are reviewed externally, or in the case of wʻenzhen, examined internally by interviewing the patient instead.

By far the most important of these various inspections that Chinese healers perform is the examination of the patient's tongue. Next would come a study of the person's pulse, probably followed by an investigation of his or her fingertips. And were these things to be done in ancient China, there would probably be an examination of the soles of the feet as well. China is where foot reflexology had its primitive origins.

A skillful Oriental doctor will also usually look for any striking superficial alteration on the surface of the patient's body, with particular attention being paid to the eyes and ears, the teeth and gums, and the head and neck in general. Likewise would visual examination of the person's bodily motions and gestures ("Body English"), general demeanor, and bodily secretions be included in wangzhen.

The objects of the doctor's wénzhen (note the direction of this accent above the letter "e", as compared to the reverse for wʻenzhen) would include the patient's tone of voice and manner of speaking, as well as the sound of his breathing, plus belching, coughing, hiccuping, and other audible symptoms of distress. And wherever present, the smell of his breath, sweat (and other bodily secretions), and even the smell of the air in the sickroom would also be included.

W'enzhen or direct questioning of the patient, can provide the health care worker with pertinent information about specific pains and functional disorders (insomnia, depressed appetite, hearing impairment, irregular menstrual periods) that might not otherwise be apparent. Previously, some exceptionally skilled and finely attuned healers were able to actually penetrate their patients' minds telepathically, provided the others were at the same level of peace and harmony as their doctors were. But this art, unfortunately, became lost in the course of time as Chinese culture grew more sophisticated in its material advancements.

Last of all, qiezhen is mostly accomplished by examining the relevant impulse points and taking the patient's pulse, which is the most important, as well as generally the last, of these procedures to be carried out. In ancient times, the soles of the feet were also pushed at various impulse points to determine the inherent strengths or weaknesses of particular organs. But this science faded away in the course of time and, ironically enough, was picked up in some Western cultures many centuries later. In due time it was refined by both the Europeans and the Americans.

BODY ENGLISH: Chinese doctors have known for a very long time that the manner in which a patient assumes different parts of his body for varying lengths of time says a lot about his or her inner emotions and thoughts. Constant fidgeting may indicate obvious nervousness; taut neck and facial muscles could be a sign of suppressed stress, like anger for example; continual sideways darting of the eyes might suggest fear or mistrust, while downcast looks may intimate low self-esteem and possible depression; a weak handshake may signify lack of determination or self-will. Briefly stated, the motions someone puts his or her body through, every few seconds or couple of minutes, says a lot about the character of the spirit within.

DIRECT QUESTIONING: As one who studies cultures from an anthropological perspective, I have had the good fortune to have observed the "direct questioning" techniques of several types of Oriental healers in my lifetime. My first encounter was with Ding Huai-ren, director of the acupuncture ward at the Soochow Chinese Medicine Hospital in Soochow, PRC, in the summer of 1980. In climbing the sacred Mount Tai near the city of Taishan (Shantung Province), my right knee had become so severely inflamed and stiff that I could barely walk, and then only with the greatest of difficulty. At the time I was touring the People's Republic of China with the American Medical Students' Association, acting in an advisory faculty capacity to some 29 American medical students.

In Soochow, I quickly discovered I could proceed no further until I had obtained some relief to a growing medical problem. In attempting to climb some stairs in the local hospital with others in our group, I suddenly fell down and laid there in terrific pain. Through an interpreter, I asked for an acupuncturist specialist to come quickly to my aid, and this is about when Ding showed up; he was one of their best, I was informed.

After doing an external physical exam of my knee, he proceeded to conduct an oral interview with me, there on the stairwell, through my interpreter. He asked me many questions about Mount Tai, how I enjoyed my trip there, how long I was there, the weather conditions at the time, the reception I received from those I met along the way, what I was fed, how I slept at night, and so forth. It was probably the most comprehensive interview I have ever had in my life.

The majority of his questions seemed more ecological or philosophical in nature than medically related to my terribly sore knee. But, as was later explained to me by another doctor present at the time, this was standard procedure for them at the time. Ding left but soon returned with some of the longest needles I believe I have ever seen stuck into human flesh. Once in my skin at various precise locations around the kneecap itself, he began twirling or gently turning the ends of each. He kept this routine up for nearly half-an-hour, at the end of which *all* pain had subsided, leaving my knee totally numb but feeling a good deal better than before. I never was bothered with that problem again. But I think his line of questioning had something to do with the healing that took place inside of me as well.

My second experience has been with my friend, Dr. Henry Yun, a Korean therapist from Seoul, who now owns and operates an East/West Wellness Center in Tijuana, Mexico. I have sat beside this man in silence and listened to him interview numerous terminally ill cancer patients.

With everyone of them he displayed amazing patience, quietly listening to their tragic and painful recitations with an understanding heart, kindly look, gentle way, and very little interruption. His soft-spoken, sometimes whispered, manner inspired within them such a strength of confidence and solidness of hope that, in some instances, just his presence could lend a remarkable healing influence by itself.

FINGERTIP ANALYSIS: The *American Journal of Physical Anthropology* (42:281, 1975; and 55:523, 1981) and *Human Heredity* (26:1-6, 1978) have published data from scientists relative to the detection of myocardial infarction in a patient's fingertips. Fingertip analysis (more properly called dermatoglyphic featuring) has proven useful in detecting numerous medical disorders, as Drs. B. Schaumann and M. Alter proved in their 1973 book *Dermatog-*

lyphics in Medical Disorders. Since then some studies of Japanese males with myocardial infarction showed a statistically significant increase in the frequency of whorls and double loop patterns in the fingertips, accompanied by decreases in ulnar loops, when compared to a similar control group without any evidence of heart disease. Significant increases in various finger specific, summed total, and absolute finger ridge counts in the heart disease subjects over those in the healthy control group was, likewise, demonstrated. Further work is being done in this area by Japanese and some Chinese scientists in order to further validate the legitimacy of this ancient but interesting method of diagnosing illnesses.

Along with this is a corresponding analysis of the fingernails. Healthy-looking nails are more often than not a sign of good health. Changes in color and appearance may sometimes be a sign of illness, but not always. Brittleness can indicate a lack of sufficient silicon; white spots may be due to a lack of adequate calcium, potassium, phosphorus, and iron in the blood; ridges usually accompany measles, mumps, pneumonia, and other serious infections; and reversal of the normal nail curvature (spoon nail) indicates a lack of iron.

Rate of nail growth is yet another way by which to gauge a few minor health problems. The nails of well-nourished people grow faster than those of the undernourished. The hand you use the most experiences the most rapid nail growth. Also, the nail of the middle finger grows fastest, while the thumbnail and little finger nail lag somewhat behind. It takes up to six months for a nail to grow from cuticle to tip.

FOOT AND HAND EXAMINATIONS: Chinese martial arts experts knew about foot and hand reflexes several thousand years ago. In both of these limbs are located certain areas that correspond to the organs, glands, and regions of the body. The science of reflexology (as it's now called) is both a diagnostic and a therapeutic tool wrapped into one. It's based on the observation that by putting a specific amount of pressure on those reflexes, you can affect the regions of the body to which they correspond. It's just that simple.

Now just about everyone enjoys a nice foot rub from time to time. Reflexology, however, isn't foot or hand massage, by any means. The ancients revered the feet and gave great attention to the feet of their invited guests. The *Bible* is replete with numerous instances of this, especially in the New Testament portion (John 13:5-14; Luke 7:37-46; 1 Timothy 5:10).

The diagnostic part comes early on, when the soles of the feet and the palms of the hands are gently pressed with the tip of one thumb. If the person upon whom this is being done lets out a yelp of pain or displays a facial grimace of any kind, the area which has just been touched indicates a corresponding organ that's in bad shape some-where within the body. The therapeutic part is basically the same routine, only more of it for longer periods on a daily basis until the problem becomes corrected or, more accurately, the particular troubled organ made well again.

In all of nature, parts reflect their whole; the same principle applies equally with the feet. Our feet comprise the only obvious horizontal bony structures of the body; they are a condensed story of the body whole. The foot resembles the form of our body. The rounded heel corresponds to our rounded buttocks. The narrow middle part of the foot corresponds to our waist. And each toe has its own narrow neck and bulbous head, as it were.

The beauty of hand and foot reflexology is its utter simplicity. If you know right/left, up/down, inner/outer, you can apply this twin diagnostic-therapeutic system to your own body in order to get results. (It's best, however, to have a friend or relative do your feet). An understanding of physiology is helpful, but not essential. If there is discomfort in the lower left part of the body, one searches out the likely tenderness in the lower part of the left foot. (Be assured that the tenderness is always there)! If there is pain in the lower right back near the spine, one works on the reflex area for the lower spine on the right foot. Detection and treatment are on the way in no time at all. How much simpler could you get than this?

The same things apply to each hand as well. There are similar reflex connections to certain internal body parts. For instance, your head reflexes are at the top of the fingers, just as the head is at the top of the body, while the wrist area corresponds very nicely to our bottom back tail bone.

There are three basic ways of applying the pressure necessary for reflexology. One is by "thumb walking," where the upper half of your thumb "walks" across the reflex area, like a crawling inch-worm might. To do this, just push down near the thumb's middle joint and roll forward to the tip. Next comes "finger walking," which is similar to thumb walking, but done with the last segment of a finger. Finally, we have "thumb hooking," where direct pres-sure is applied to a certain reflex point by pushing straight down with the tip of a thumb or finger.

How much pressure should be used in foot or hand reflexology? This cannot be described, only experienced from constant practice on yourself and others. Basically, you ought to use medium thumb pressure. Since each person requires a different level of pressure, the one administering said therapies should be sensitive to the recipient's needs.

It's okay for the recipient to feel an *occasional* "good hurt," but the treatment should never be painfully excruciating, by any means. Ask for feedback from your recipient as you proceed, in order to determine just how much pressure ought to be applied. And bear this in mind as you're working on the individual's feet or hands: too much pressure can damage fragile blood vessels or cause other problems.

Sometimes when the thumbs become tired, a simple tool can be resorted to, such as the eraser tip of a pencil.

But be careful not to apply too much pressure with this particular instrument. Also, the knuckles can be used to give the thumbs a brief rest, but here again beware of the pressure you're exerting. Reflexology is best done without the benefit of creams, lotions, or oils, so as to preserve your sensitivity.

ODOR SNIFFING: Many ancient and modern Oriental healers still resort to the common practice of sniffing their patients' urine, stools, sweat, breath, armpits, and so forth. From these several different substances or body parts can they learn a lot about an individual's personal state of health. I remember one Chinese doctor in Singapore some years ago who sniffed my breath, beneath my arms, my palms, and the soles of my feet before concluding that my two major problems at that time were poor digestion and an over-worked liver. These were the identical dysfunctions which a licensed medical doctor and a naturopathic physician had both identified earlier here in the U.S. Yet this humble and wizened old man, without any benefits whatsoever of a high school or college education and sophisticated medical equipment, surmised the same things just using his nose and wisdom.

He reminded me in halting English how animals often sniffed each other. When was the last time I had a strange dog come up to me and sniff between my legs in the groin area, he wondered aloud. Surely this thing, he felt, indicated a usefulness in the animal kingdom and with mankind, too. Suffice it to say, he never once sneezed while sniffing me, like the German shepherd did some years before that!

PULSE TAKING: Pulse diagnosis represents over 2,000 years of clinical experience distilled, clarified, and refined for the benefit of today's patients and student practitioners. This is a process that could scarcely be duplicated from the beginning in the course of a single lifetime, let alone hastily reconstructed by means of a few weeks' or months' instruction. It's somewhat similar to that of learning Braille—in both cases the student must cultivate the sensitivity of his or her fingertips, learn to make very subtle tactile distinctions and then interpret these distinctions as meaningful bits of information.

So just as the student of Braille will have already thoroughly assimilated the grammar and vocabulary of his own language, and even as the beginning violinist can distinguish a melody from a random assemblage of sounds, in the same way the student practitioner of pulse diagnosis should have by now mastered the rational discipline of it as well as the underlying medical theory before attempting to acquire the technical skills involved. Only then will he really know what to look for in a patient's pulse, and only then will he realize what he has found when he discovers it.

Oriental and European doctors, with many years of proficiency in this diagnostic skill, will tell you that a real mastery of it requires an extended period of practical, hands-on instruction— just as one can hardly learn to read Braille by simply memorizing a printed card with a list of characters overnight. All that is necessary, it seems, for correct pulse diagnosis is a set of fingertips that haven't been desensitized by too much manual labor.

Even a few hours of tennis, rowing, or puttering around the yard are enough to desensitize one's fingers for quite awhile. Also, pulse diagnosis is just as objective and verifiable, when done right, as a blind man's ability to read a Braille text correctly by passing his fingers over it enough times.

Pulse diagnosis had its real origins in the prudery of Chinese doctors to examine their patients (especially the females) fully clothed. Modesty was a strong point in ancient Oriental cultures, and one seldom ever finds the naked human form represented in classical Chinese artwork. Female patients would extend a bare forearm from behind a curtain or panel, and from this the physician was expected to diagnose and treat from pulse clues alone.

Pulse diagnosis is believed to be at least 4,000 years old. It's mentioned in the oldest Chinese medical text, the *Nei Ching Su Wen*, which has been attributed to the Yellow Emperor, who ascended the throne in the year 2698 B.C., it's believed. But as Oriental medical expert and practicing doctor, Ted Kapthchuk noted in his book, *The Web That Has No Weaver: Understanding Chinese Medicine*, the Chinese held no special monopoly on pulse diagnosis. For we find the great Roman physician Galen (129-200 A.D.) describing over 100 different pulse types in his writings, differentiating size, strength, speed, duration of diastole and/or systole, frequency, and hardness or softness. For the most part, however, pulse diagnosis appears to have become a lost art in the West, although it's still an important part of any self-respecting Chinese medicine practitioner's method of diagnosis.

While pulse diagnosis takes many years of experience to become expert at, as mentioned before, even beginners can make reasonable diagnoses of simple health problems after just a few months of intensive study. The first rule for the practitioner to abide by is that he or she must be at peace with himself or herself. For as the Yellow

Emperor told his Health Minister Ch'i Po in the *Nei Ching*: "When man is serene and healthy, the pulse of the heart flows and connects, just as pearls are joined together or like a string of red jade; then one can speak of a healthy heart." Hostile feelings or a depressed mood have no place in an Oriental-trained practitioner when he or she is about to make a pulse diagnosis of another person. The feelings must be positive and the mood pleasant in order to detect the subtlest changes in the patient's pulse; otherwise, an incorrect diagnosis will be made more often than not.

A simple introduction here should enable you, the reader, to recognize some of the simplest health clues to be found in the pulse. The pulse will reveal what are called depth of illness, internal temperature, and function of internal organs. Depth of illness is indicated by the location of the pulse, whether it's superficial or deep against the bone. Internal temperature is shown by the speed of the pulse. Function of internal organs refers to the relationship between the condition of specific organs and pulse positions. Each time you feel for a pulse, keep in mind these three factors: depth, speed, and organ. One last factor is quality, a subjective interpretation of the overall pulse that helps pinpoint diagnosis further.

One of the best places to start is with your own pulse. The three most important pulse points are to be found on the wrist or, to be more precise, along the radial artery just in front of, directly over, and behind the styloides radii. This location is called the ostium pollicare, cunkou in Chinese; both mean the "opening of the thumb. There are also three radial pulse points on each hand, within proximity of the thumb."

Feel along the edge of your wrist for the bony protuberance just below your thumb. This is the styloid process of your radius. Feel for the pulse with your first three fingers, placing your middle finger directly behind the styloid. The other two fingers snuggle across the wrist to each side, touching the middle finger.

When you begin feeling another person's pulse, be aware of the size of the other's hand relative to your own. If the person's hand is much larger than yours, spread your fingers a little as you place them on the radial artery. If the hand is much smaller than yours, place your three fingers tightly together. Always place the middle finger in position first. Now you're ready to seek clues as to depth, speed, organ, and quality.

A normal pulse can be felt distinctly at a medium depth and remains distinct at the deepest depth. If you happen to get a cold or flu, you'll most likely be able to detect your own pulse at the most superficial level by barely touching your skin. This is referred to as a floating pulse and usually fades under great pressure. It generally appears with acute lung-related symptoms.

Deep pulses, on the other hand, are those felt only under great pressure. They indicate chronic problems which have lodged somewhere within the center of the body. The significance of this differentiation between superficial and deep pulses depends on the Chinese belief of depths to sickness. At first, disease strikes the external levels of our immune system, and if we are weak, we suffer exterior kinds of illness like a cold or flu. But if our inner defenses are similarly down, then the sickness tends to move inward, striking much deeper in our bodies until it becomes firmly lodged and is more difficult to cure. Obese folks usually have deeper pulses, while leaner ones have pulses that feel "larger" than normal.

The pulse, along with certain symptoms, gives the correct diagnosis and suggests the best treatment. As you hold your own pulse, take a full inhalation and let it out. Now begin to count how many beats occur between the next normal inhalation and exhalation.

If you are healthy, you should be able to count either four or five pulses to each complete breath (one cycle of inhalation and exhalation). If your condition is due to heat, you will count six or more beats, i.e., the pulse will be too fast. Rapid pulses often accompany symptoms such as frequent thirst, rashes, a desire for cold drinks, infrequent urination, constipation, a yellowish coating on your tongue, and/or a tendency to bruise or to bleed from the gums (heat injures the small blood vessels, according to Chinese theory).

If your condition is due to invasion of cold, your pulse will be three beats or less per complete breath, i.e., too slow. You undoubtedly prefer hot drinks over cold ones, like to wear more clothing and use more blankets than others do, have poor circulation, loose bowels, feel fatigued, and have a white coating on the tongue. Bear in mind that athletes have normally slower pulses than others, and children have normally faster pulses than adults do.

The ancient Chinese discovered that each finger on the pulse was a window to a specific organ. They considered the heart, lungs, spleen-stomach, liver, and kidneys the major organs of the body. Each is paired in function and dysfunction with another organ, in an ever-more complicated system of interaction. By testing the pulse, a practitioner can decipher the health of the small intestine, large intestine, stomach, gall bladder, and urinary bladder, as well as the major organs.

Beginning with your left wrist, the number one position is the index finger, which represents the heart. Number two (the middle finger) indicates the liver, and number three (the ring finger) is the level of inborn life force, called qi or chi, in the kidney. On the right wrist, number one is the lung, number two is the spleen-stomach, and number three is the quality of kidney function.

Up to now you have discovered the depth of your pulse and its speed. Let us now assume you feel the pulse on your left wrist. After you concentrate on feeling the pulse beating against all three of your fingers, lift up the ring and middle fingers so all you feel is the pulse against your index finger. Put down the middle finger and lift up the index finger. Notice any difference in intensity between the two pulses. Now place the ring finger on the pulse and lift the middle finger. Observe this pulse alone. Go back and forth a few times, feeling each of the three positions individually to reveal any discrepancies in strength. For instance, the kidney energy pulse in older people is often noticeably weaker than the others. The Chinese believe this energy is inborn and is dissipated with each passing year.

Now switch to your right wrist. Follow the same routine, first feeling the pulse clearly against all three fingers, noticing any differences there. Then, lift up the fingers so you can concentrate on one position at a time, and compare the three of them. Let's assume for a moment that the pulse beneath your middle finger is popping the strongest or weakest of the three. Are you suffering a lot of gas, bloating, or digestion? The middle position on the wrist relates to spleen-stomach.

Following is a table of the functions of the five organs you should be diagnosing on yourself. You will observe some radical differences between Western and ancient Chinese physiological concepts:

Heart: relates to blood and blood vessels, happiness and laughter, the tongue, and mental illness or spiritual discord.

Lung: relates to moistening the body, sadness and crying, the nose, and the skin.

Spleen: relates to digestion, contemplation, muscle tone, the mouth, and the holding of organs in place (such as preventing the prolapses of colon or uterus, for instance).

Liver: relates to menstruation, anger, the eyes, the fingernails, the movement of energy around the body, and the movement of muscles and joints.

Kidney: relates to growth and development of the body in general and the sexual organs in particular, fear, bones, bone marrow, head hair, water metabolism, the back, and the body's inherent levels of energy and warmth.

An imbalance of energy (qi) at one of these pulse sites could relate to any of the above functions of the associated organ.

The quality of the pulse is probably the most difficult aspect to determine, considering that the experts differentiate over 20 nuances. To make it simple, the reader is advised to stay with just the three main pulse categories: slippery, wiry, and thready.

A slippery pulse feels like marbles rolling around a plate just beneath the skin surface. The best way to sensitize yourself to the feeling of a slippery pulse is to feel the pulse of an expectant mother, since pregnancy often leads to this type of pulse. Slippery pulse can, in the absence of childbearing, also indicate a menstrual period or internal dampness, as in sluggish digestion, mucus, and some types of joint stiffness and pain.

A wiry pulse feels like a guitar string flopping against your fingers. This kind of pulse is firm, tight, and clipped. It points to liver dysfunction more than anything else, as a rule. By referring to the aforementioned table of particular organ functions, you can see that a wiry pulse may be associated with menstrual problems, spasms, eye complaints, and stagnant (qi) energy, as in tumors, nodules, and dull aches.

Thready pulses feel like a thin thread beating mildly against your fingers. Thready pulse signifies blood deficiency and is associated with pale skin, dizziness, blurred vision, numb extremities, and sometimes insomnia.

Some Chinese doctors believe that a woman's pulses are naturally stronger on the right wrist, while those of a man's are strongest on the left side. This has led to the conclusion that you can often correctly discern the sex of an unborn child by simply feeling which wrist of the expectant mother registers the strongest pulse. If her right side is stronger, then it should be a girl; if the left, then a boy.

Several good books to read on the subject are listed below. They should enable you to become even more proficient on pulse diagnosis after awhile. But remember, just like with a blind man reading Braille, it takes years to master the subject thoroughly.

Li Shi Zhen. *Pulse Diagnosis* (Paradigm Publications, 1985).

Ted. I. Kapthuck. *The Web That Has No Weaver* (Congdon & Weed, 1984).

SOUND DETECTION: A doctor uses a stethoscope to magnify the respiratory and cardiac sounds in the chest of his patient that he may wish to listen to. But just a good ear and a little training can enable a person to hear other types of sounds, which the body frequently makes, that could indicate a variety of different problems. Among these might be the following.

Belching, reported the late physician, Henry G. Bieler, M.D. in his book, *Food Is Your Best Medicine*, is comparable to the voice of the conscience; only in this case, it's located in the solar plexus. He says such a distress signal originates from the body when a person overeats, when there is an incompatible combination of foods, or when there is inadequate digestion. He said we need to heed this warning of nature more often.

Farting (or the emission of intestinal gas from the rectum) is a sure indication of undigested foods and inadequate bowel movements. However, the consumption of certain foods, like beans, can lead to this as well.

Stomach growling and similar noises occurring within the abdomen may be an indication of hunger, or an over consumption of food, or indigestion.

Ringing in the ears could mean nervousness, head problems, medication side-effects, or even ear infection, if one's full-time occupation doesn't happen to be as a bellringer in the lofty steeple of a huge cathedral somewhere.

A raspy voice which cackles like that of an old witch might indicate severe throat infection in some cases.

A wheezing of the lungs could suggest that the individual is asthmatic, suffering from bronchitis or emphysema, or allergic to something in the air.

There are other examples besides those which have been cited here, but these should suffice for the time being. Becoming intimately familiar with your body will enable you to know it inside and out. In no time at all, you should be well enough acquainted with all of its peculiar little quirks, including the many strange sounds it makes every so often. For they are indications as to just how well or poorly it's doing internally.

TELEPATHIC COMMUNICATION: In ancient China, some practitioners who were in perfect control of their thoughts and emotions were able to discern their patients' own feelings simply by "tuning in" to them. But in order for this to be successfully accomplished, there had to be absolute tranquility in the minds and hearts of both healer and patient alike. Only then could perfect mental telepathy between both parties be possible. Such a silent flow of ideas and feelings involved constant eye contact between the two, besides the mind and heart of each. Today, this ability is virtually nonexistent, even in China where it originated several millenniums ago. How nice it will be, though, when the time again comes that the healer, merely by looking at his or her patient, can detect with the eyes and discern with the mind what is troubling the other without a verbal explanation of the same.

TONGUE DIAGNOSIS: According to ancient Oriental medical thought, the tongue had its roots in the heart; therefore, interpretation of it is important in discerning the health of the heart, blood, and liver. All aspects of the surface of the tongue are useful in forming an understanding.

The mucus coloration and textures of this mucus tell us of temporary or changing conditions. Coloration of mucus portrays impending disturbances and determines whether the disease is in the first, second, or deepest stages of expression. For instance, a white, shiny mucus coat can indicate the beginnings of a cold; as it becomes more yellow it lets us know that the stomach is somehow involved. The coloration becomes grey-white as the condition reaches deeper involvement. A healthy tongue should always be a pale, red color.

Examine the shape of the tongue. It shouldn't appear to be swollen, nor should it be too thin. It should be flexible when extended, and the surface of the tongue should be ulcer free.

Wet or dry textures tell us other things about the internal health of the body in general. A pale, excessively moist, and slightly swollen tongue usually indicates a digestive problem. Additional symptoms may include constant fatigue and feeling chilled all the time. If the mucus coat on the tongue is wet, slippery, and profuse, then a good ginger root foot bath is recommended.

A ginger foot bath is made by placing one large grated or mashed fresh root of ginger in a two-quart pan of very hot water. One-third part of apple cider vinegar is then added. The water must be so hot that it's almost unbearable. The person sits covered with a blanket with his or her feet immersed for 20 minutes, two or three times a day. If the water cools, more hot water must be added. A warming tea can also be made of equal parts of yarrow, lemon balm, vervain and catnip (two tablespoons per cup of hot water), let steep one-two hours. Drink hot, two-three cups daily.

If during the onset of a sickness the mucus coat is dry, furred and either white or yellow, this suggests that there is an internal fever somewhere or indigestion. If the tongue is dry, thin, and pale, it usually indicates problems relating to the blood or the heart such as menstrual problems in women or palpitations. Other symptoms may include insomnia and feelings of dullness. A tongue that is too red and very dry, along with a yellow coating, suggests possible emotional problems like repressed anger or resentment. Physical symptoms include headaches, constant thirst, constipation, and poor sleep patterns.

A simple coolant is called for in such cases as these. Squeeze half of a cut lime into an eight fluid ounce glass of lukewarm water. And a good herbal infusion to use is equal parts of the roots of wild yam, comfrey, and dandelion, along with crushed cumin seeds. Use two tablespoonfuls per boiling cup of water, covered and steeped an hour, then drink lukewarm after straining. Also recommended are hot and cold showers half-a-dozen times in succession, alternating between both temperatures but ending with a cold one. This procedure can be repeated three or four times daily as needed.

Lines or creases indicate an injured organ somewhere in the body. Like the iris of the eye, the lines and shape of the tongue serve as a record keeper. A line cutting the surface of the tongue must be caused by something major or long standing. If the tongue has no coating to speak of, but has a crack running down the center of it and is extremely red and irritated, know then that your stomach and kidneys may be in bad shape. It also suggests a definite lack of the B-complex vitamins.

Coloration of the tongue itself, which was cited earlier in this text, is a good indication of the condition of the blood stream. A vibrant light pink color indicates good quality of blood and circulation. When looking at the tongue, the color should come out at you. If you have to look for the color you know the blood is deficient. A washed-out color indicates anemia; more bluish, poor circulation. A gray color indicates poor oxygenation of the blood. Pollutants such as arsenic, carbon monoxide, and nicotine may make the tongue gray.

The size of the tongue indicates the quality and tone of the heart. Very large tongues (relative to the size of the mouth) can indicate atony, water kidneys, fatty heart, or as simple a condition as athlete's heart (hypertrophy of this muscle due to overindulgence in sports). A shriveled, thin tongue indicates a weak, exhausted heart.

Always be sure to cross-check tongue diagnosis with other systems of analysis, for each one focuses the other and reinforces a correct evaluation. The primary systems of diagnosis to cross-check with are iridology, facial color and lines, muscle testing, and plain, old intuition (which may or may not be an insipid form of telepathic communication). Some secondary diagnostic systems to serve as backup cross-checks with tongue analysis are nails, pulse, palm, external marking, and reflexology. Recommended reading is Willima LeSassier's book entitled *Natural Diagnosis, A Way of Listening* (1978).

Herbal Cures

In 1933 the world's oldest man died at the incredible age of 256! His name was Dr. Li Chung Yun. With great fanfare *The New York Times*, the *Toronto Globe*, and other major metropolitan dailies around the world, heralded his passing. Dr. Yun had outlived 23 wives and was living with his 24th at the time of his demise.

In his first century of life, he knew practically nothing about good eating habits, vitamins, calories, or exercise. It was then he decided to change some of his old habits and implement new ways of living. By the time he had reached his second century of life, he decided to go public with some of his unique herbal formulas that had kept him going all of these many, many years. He gave 28 lectures at a Chinese university at the age of 207 on his secrets of staying well and living a long, long time. Each lecture lasted up to three hours, it is said.

In the West aging men often boast of their years, slyly adding a few birthdays, but it was different with Li Chung Yun, who appears to have cheated in the other direction! A professor in the Minkuo University claims to have found records showing that Li was born in 1677, and that on his 150th birthday and 200th birthday he had been congratulated by the Chinese government. Men who are old today declare that their great-grandfathers, as boys, knew Li as a grown man.

Early in life—either about 1690, 1750, or thereabouts—Li Chung Yun developed a penchant for collecting herbs, a habit that continued for over a century. Li Chung Yun also understood that it was the part of wisdom to keep a quiet heart, sit like a tortoise, walk sprightly like a pigeon, and sleep like a dog. But that is merely camouflage. There are people without number today who have the tortoise temperament and whom it is almost impossible to awaken in the morning, but they pass on without any notice in cable dispatches. Walking sprightly like a pigeon is among the arts lost by man, and it may be that loss of his favorite herb led to Li's untimely taking off; which is a discouraging conclusion to the life story of a calm Oriental who watched the centuries come and go.

What were three of Dr. Yun's favorite herbs? Why, foo-ti-teng, gotu kola, and heavenly grade ginseng root. He would drink two different "Elixirs of Life," as he liked to call them, alternating them every other day. The common ingredient in both was gotu kola, with heavenly grade ginseng root being in one of them and foo-ti-teng being in the other. This switching around seemed to work well for him. On even-numbered days of the calendar he would drink his ginseng-gotu kola tonic in the morning and again in the evening, and on odd-numbered days he would resort to the foo-ti-teng and gotu kola tonic twice daily.

He discovered that by doing this for a century or more he kept his circulation up, his mental clarity active, his vision good, his heart sound, and his soul happy. Now he just didn't use any old ordinary grades of ginseng, foo-ti-teng or gotu kola, but particular species of these plants.

In time he also formulated a number of other useful herbal combinations for men and women of all ages. This data he passed on to his audiences whenever he gave lengthy public lectures on health and longevity in general. Such valuable information would have passed into obscurity had it not been for the fact that some of his numerous posterity got in touch with a Canadian importer some years ago, and finally brought all of these many excellent products to the market place. Through Leo Albi and his company Albi Imports Ltd., of Burnaby, British Columbia, the descendants of this renowned double centenarian were at last able to make their grandfather's formulas available to the public.

Ironically enough, Li Chung Yun's formulas have been the best kept secret of most North American Chinese herb shops for the last several decades or so. Only recently have regular health food stores and nutrition centers become aware of them. A few have started stocking them, but most still do not. Several Vancouver, B.C., naturopathic doctors were accidentally alerted to these wonderful products by several of their Oriental patients, who had been taking some of them for years. The doctors subsequently bought some for themselves and recommended them to fellow naturopaths in the states; soon there was a growing demand for them in the Northwest.

Today, Albi Imports Ltd. are the sole distributors of Dr. Yun's herb line, some of which helped him to live to be 256 years of age. Those wishing to contact this company for more information about these wonderful, life-giving products can do so at one of the following addresses:

ALBI IMPORTS LIMITED
7188 Curragh Ave.
Burnaby, B.C. VSJ 4V9
(604)-438-2029

ALBI IMPORTS LIMITED
Unit B, Bldg. C, Colony Park
19029 6th Ave. West
Lynnwood, WA. 98036
(206)-778-9494

What follows is a brief listing of all of Dr. Yun's remarkable longevity and total health formulas, and short descriptions about the functions of each:

Li Chung Yun's Herbal Formulas

HEAVENLY GRADE KOREAN GINSENG: (Tea, Extract, Powder, Capsules, Tablets): There are three grades of this kind of ginseng—heaven, earth, and man grades—with heaven being the highest and purest of all. Much has been written in the medical and scientific literature about ginseng, so only a few lines can be devoted to it here. Ginseng affects sugar metabolism. One component, ginsenin, acts somewhat like insulin does in the body. Another important constituent, panoxic acid, regulates the metabolism and functioning of the cardiovascular system and prevents cholesterol buildup as well. Panaxin, a third ingredient in ginseng root, stimulates the central nervous and cardiovascular systems directly. Panaquilon, a fourth component, affects the entire endocrine gland system, most likely at the hypothalmic and pituitary levels.

The assorted volatile oils in the root have a direct relationship with the brain in terms of increasing mental alertness. Ginseng root has numerous steroids which are responsible for many of its effects. These steroids are similar in some ways to the human sex hormones testosterone and estrogen, as well as being related to cortisol (cortisone) and other adrenalcortical hormones. The adrenal hormones regulate many of our most important metabolic and adaptive functions.

Ginseng also contains what are known as ginsenosides. Behavioral studies in rats have demonstrated that some of them can decrease fatigue and promote learning in rodents. Soviet studies confirm that they increased the weight of the testicles in male animal models. Japanese research confirmed that the root can increase the number of active sperm in male animals and humans. Ginseng has become a prime example of an adaptogenic agent.

A great deal of research has demonstrated that animals given ginseng as a regular part of their diet were able to function normally, or more normally, under stressful conditions than did animals fed normal diets but without the benefits of this herb. Animals consistently fed ginseng outperform animals not fed the root and can survive under conditions normally intolerable to that species. Ginseng seems to relieve what is known as the "stress syndrome" which occurs after prolonged stress of either physical or mental origin.

Experimental animals given ginseng didn't develop enlarged adrenals (a dangerous sign), hypertension, neurosis, or deficiency of Vitamin C in the adrenals even when exposed to stresses that normally would cause these reactions. And such animals fed ginseng hadsignificantly greater physical endurance than animals fed a normal diet but no ginseng. Lab animals fed ginseng have been shown to outlive animals not fed ginseng by 14% of a lifetime.

FOO-TI-TENG: This is one of Dr. Yun's three favorite herbs. It contains almost 50% carbohydrates, which explains its wonderful energy-boosting properties. Some Indian and European psychiatrists have reported that many of their elderly patients who've taken foo-ti-teng regularly have experienced greater mental clarity and depressed senility as a result of this. One French biochemist discovered that new brain and nerve cells grew in place of the old, deteriorated ones when foo-ti-teng was fed to animal models (rhesus monkeys) for up to six months or more. Speaking of this plant in his book, *The Way of Herbs*, practicing herbalist Michael Tierra of Santa Cruz, California. noted that "it plays an important role in the treatment of all deficiency diseases."

GOTU KOLA: This is a prolific weed growing throughout much of Southeast Asia. Attempts to cultivate it in gardens prove futile; but just throw some seeds on the ground, repeatedly walk or drive a truck over the spot, virtually neglect them, and watch them grow like mad! *Medicinal Plants of the Philippines* (p. 685) by Eduardo

Quisumbing, reported that gotu kola is "very rich in Vitamin B." Some of the B-complex vitamins, like niacin and inositol, are vital for the functioning of the brain. Some years ago, an Indian physician by the name of Dr. M.V.R. Appa Rao administered an extract of gotu kola to a number of retarded children in Madras with surprising results.

As later reported in the *Journal of Research in Indian Medicine* (8:4, 1973), most of these children started scoring much higher on I.Q. tests, displayed increased attention span, and retained what they learned longer than before taking the gotu kola. Little wonder then, that Li Chung Yun stayed so mentally alert for 256 years simply by taking his daily dose of gotu kola, along with alternating amounts of ginseng and foo-ti-teng!

GINKGO BILOBA: For some five millenniums, Chinese herbalists have been using an extract made from fresh green leaves of the ginkgo biloba tree, one of the world's oldest living species of trees. According to the September 15, 1967 issue of *Science* (157:1270-72) journal, gingkos have probably existed on earth longer than any other tree that is now living. Charles Darwin, the famous evolutionist, characterized them as incredible living fossils. The ginkgo tree is the sole surviving species of the group of plants known as Ginkgoales, whose ancestry has been traced back more than 200 million years. Ginkgos evolved from ancient seed ferns in Permian times and somehow managed to survive the great catastrophic upheavals of the earth (volcanos, earthquakes, glaciers) during the Tertiary and Quaternary periods. Not even the mighty dinosaurs had such staying power as these unique trees did!

I discovered an intriguing report on ginkgo biloba in a back issue of *Clinical Trial Journal* (22:149-57, 1985) not too long ago. What really caught my attention, though, was that this report covered research that involved 112 geriatric patients. These people had diagnoses of chronic cerebral insufficiency. For younger people looking for something of future value, or a product they can use as a preventive if they have developed early symptoms, or if they have older family members in their households, this may be of definite interest to them. The symptoms projected by the 112 individuals in the trial included ringing in the ears, depression, lack of vigilance, short-term memory loss, vertigo, and headaches.

Although not all of the 112 patients studied had all of the symptoms, most of them had the majority of them—enough, at least, to make a valid test. The article also pointed out that numerous Americans have symptoms of decreased cerebral blood flow. It's a common problem, and can be dangerous if left unattended. This can be due to the high rate of cardiovascular disease in America.

According to the testing, the gingko biloba appeared to increase cerebral blood flow, which produced an increase in oxygen. An added dividend was better utilization of glucose which is classed as a brain food. The extract also produced an effect on blood platelets by reducing the clotting effect, thus providing good protection against stroke.

What made me really feel good about this remedy was that there do not seem to be any kind of side effects from it. Researchers claimed that the results of the year-long study using this particular material at 40 mg. (3 times daily) was a statistically significant regression of all the major symptoms. No wonder that Dr. Li Chung Yun lived for two and a half centuries in apparently the best of health, thanks to his frequent intake of ginkgo!

A leading conservative French medical magazine, *La Presse Medicale*, carried ten separate reports in its September 25, 1986 issue relative to memory improvement and enhanced brain function from ginkgo. The ginkgo which Albi Imports distributes contains 24% leaf extract, the highest amount possible in the herb industry. Recommended intake is generally three capsules daily.

REISHI MUSHROOM: I met a professional acquaintance of mine, Terry Willard, a Canadian herbalist based in Calgary, not too long ago at a Canadian Health Food Association convention in Toronto (1990). He told me that, in a computer search for scientific papers published on reishi (also called ganoderma or fu zheng), he eventually came up with well over 200 papers that dated from 1969 to 1989. The majority of these papers show the following proven health benefits for this wonderful medicinal mushroom:

The RNA from it disrupts viral disease processes inducing interferon production.

Reishi inhibits nasty bacteria like staphylococcus, streptococcus, and pneuominiae.

In Japan, the government recognizes reishi as an official substance for the natural treatment of cancer.

Reishi reduces blood fat levels, including "bad" (LDL) cholesterol.

Reishi improved 81.77% of heart disease patients in nine Chinese hospitals.

In 48% of heart disease patients, reishi produced marked improvement, and in 86% a general improvement.

Reishi lowers high blood pressure nicely.

Reishi alleviates allergies.

Reishi provided relief to 60%-90% of chronic bronchitis sufferers; older patients experienced greater relief.

Reishi also alleviates food sensitivities.

DANG QUAI: The root reduces hypertension, slows down the pulse rate, and relaxes the cardiac muscle in middle-aged to elderly men and women. Lab testing has demonstrated dang quei's bactericidal action against such bacteria as dysentery and staphylococcus. Extracts of this root have shown in vitro and in vivo antiviral and antifungal activities. It's also of medical value in stabilizing blood sugar levels. The root works well with vitamin E and improves the absorption and utilization of this nutrient within the body.

LICORICE ROOT: Manifests a neutral kind of energy and enters all twelve acupuncture meridians, but seems especially beneficial to the spleen, stomach, kidney, and lungs. It supplements the energy forces within us and strikes a happy balance with some of our major internal organs. It tends to drive out all poisons and toxins from the system and to eliminate side effects from other herbs and supplements. Licorice root cleans out the meridian pathways and allows Chi energy to flow smoothly through them.

And important point to remember here is that Chinese licorice root (Glycyrrhizae uralensis) is quite different from the Western species (Glycyrrhizae glabra). The latter tends to make people nervous when taken in excess; but the Chinese kind delivers a smooth, calm sort of energy, irregardless of how much is taken. So don't confuse Western licorice root with the kind that Dr. Yun periodically took to stay fit and trim for all of his 256 years of life.

KONJAC ROOT (GLUCOMANNAN): A particular polysaccharide of tremendous value in weight loss and constipation. It's obtained from the tubers of Amorphophallus rivieri or konjac, a perennial plant widely cultivated from Indonesia to Japan. The root is used in the preparation of konjaku flour; further processing of the flour yields glucomannan. Glucomannan swells tremendously when it comes in contact with water; it expands to about 60 times its original volume when consumed. This increased bulk in the stomach produces a feeling of fullness so people are inclined to eat less; and it makes for a fast-acting bulk laxative, too.

HERBAL LAXATIVE #1: Contains senna, cascara sagrada, licorice and rhubarb roots, and buckthorn. This formula has been giving wonderful bowel movements since ancient times. A dosage of three capsules on an empty stomach is recommended.

L.B.C. #2: Contains cascara, barberry, cayenne, the roots of ginger, golden seal and rhubarb, lobelia, red raspberry and fennel. Tonifies the entire G.I. tract and colon. Take two capsules daily with meals.

SUPER COMPOUND #3: Contains ginseng (Korean and Siberian), foo-ti-teng, gotu kola and bee pollen. Dr. Yun took this on an "as needed" basis for energy and stamina. One or two capsules daily or intermittently with meals are suggested.

PEI PA LI #4: Contains wild cherry, horehound, golden seal, cayenne, ginger, licorice, orange peel, slippery elm, and fenugreek. A natural preventive and remedial agent for colds and flus. Take three or four capsules between meals, daily, during cold and flu season.

NIRVANA #5: Contains black cohosh, valerian, passion flower, lobelia, skullcap, wood betony, lady's slipper, gotu kola, Siberian ginseng, and red clover. This old Chinese formula for relieving stress and tension has been improved with the addition of several Western herbs. Take three capsules daily on an empty stomach, as needed.

SUM YUEN LI #6: Contains hawthorn, motherwort, tienchi ginseng, mistletoe, and cayenne. This formula kept Li Chung Yun's heart and circulatory system in great shape for approximately 256 years! Take two capsules daily with meals.

A & R #7: Contains hydrangea, alfalfa, yucca, devil's claw, burdock, seaweeds (kelp and bladderwrack), skullcap, cayenne, and sarsaparilla. Intended to keep the joints and muscles limber; useful for arthritis and rheumatism. Take three capsules each day between meals, or more as needed.

K & B #8: Contains juniper, cleavers, stillengia, ho-shou-wu, uva ursi, buchu, watermelon seeds, marshmallow root. Effective for kidney and bladder functions. Take two capsules daily.

SHIGATZE "D" #9: Contains Stephania tetranda root, Poria cocus mushroom, Akebia quinata fruit and root, Morus bombycis (M. australis) (mulberry) rootbark, Perilla ocimoides (P. frutescens) plant, Polyporus umbellatus (sulphureus) Fries mushroom, and Acanthopanax spinosus root. A slow way to lose weight; but unlike the so-called "overnight wonders" that claim to "melt" the fat away only to have it come back again later on, this formula keeps the fat *off permanently*! Take two capsules an hour before meals three times daily; expect results in four to six months! But be assured that what comes off, stays off for good!

SHIGATZE TEA #10: Same slow-working but permanent weight reduction formula in tea form. Due to the acrid flavor, however, it doesn't appeal to everyone's taste buds. Brief descriptions of each of the ingredients follows:

S. tetranda root yields the alkaloid tetrandrine, which has been shown to be a muscle relaxant, anti-hypertensive agent, and metabolic and cardiac stimulant.

P. cocos mushroom grows in roots of old pine trees, about 20 to 30 centimeters underground in various tuberous shapes. Contains pure choline, one of the B-complex vitamins which is essential to lecithin formation (lecithin reduces serum cholesterol). Exhibits tranquilizing action on body metabolism, exerts diuretic influence on kidneys and bladder, and lowers blood sugar levels a bit.

A. quinata fruit seed oil contains 23% palmitic, 2% stearic, 53% oleic, and 22% linoleic acids (the first two being saturated and the latter two being unsaturated fatty acids). Linoleic is an essential fatty acid. According to R.S. Goodhart, M.D., and M.E. Shils, M.D., *Modern Nutrition in Health and Disease* (5th Ed., pp. 134; 897) such essential fatty acids are necessary for the efficient transport and metabolism of cholesterol, especially in decreasing serum cholesterol concentrations.

M. bombycis rootbark is a useful diuretic for fluid retention and exerts mild laxative action on sluggish colons.

P. ocimoides plant is employed extensively in Chinese herbal medicine to treat compulsive eating disorders on account of its "pungent, warming, sedative" qualities and is "antidotal when given for poisoning by crabs and fish [probably poisonous and spoiled food]." It's excellent for the removal of mucus from the lungs or colon.

P. umbellatus mushroom functions as a useful purgative for intestinal parasites in the Philippines. It's related to P. cocos.

A. spinosus root diminishes pain, especially that occurring in the stomach, liver, and spleen.

Most of these herbs have had their medical efficacy verified in various clinical and experimental settings by Oriental doctors in different Southeast Asian countries. When combined together they are effective in gradual and permanent weight loss.

TAU-FA YUEN #11: Contains ho-shou-wu, bladderwrack, kelp, ginseng, cayenne, and nettle. Keeps the hair from turning grey and becoming thin, if used regularly from the time when such things begin to occur. Take two capsules daily.

NATURAL HERB FIBER #12: Contains psyllium, licorice, butternut bark, black walnut, rhubarb, bentonite clay, and fennel. Designed to prevent atherosclerosis, diabetes, diverticulitis, colorectal cancer, and similar maladies induced by the consumption of refined foods. Take three capsules daily with meals.

ASTRAGALUS 8 HERBS COMBINATION #14: Contains astragalus root, ginseng (Korean and Siberian), ganoderma, echinacea, schizandra, licorice, and atractylodes. Strengthens the immune system against major viral and bacterial infections. Take two capsules daily with meals.

PO-CHAI #15: Contains atractylodes root, licorice, codonopsis root, peony root, ginger, poria mushroom, orange peel, and papaya fruit enzyme. Helps to digest food. Take one to three capsules per meal on an as-needed basis.

HY-PO #16: Contains dandelion root, licorice, cedar berries, ginger, Siberian ginseng, and acanthopanax root. Useful for low blood sugar or hypoglycemia. Take two capsules daily with meals.

"L" #1K#18: Contains dandelion, black radish, ho-shou-wu, barberry, bupleurum, peony, golden seal, ginger, and cayenne. Great liver tonic! Take two capsules daily with a meal.

ANTLER HORN 7 HERB COMBINATION #19: Contains reindeer antlers, ginseng root, and six other Oriental herbs. Stag horn consists of amino acids, peptides, cholesterol, collagen, cartilage, hartshorn spirit, and ammonium carbonate. In Chinese and Japanese traditional medicines, young deer horn is prized for its pure energy effects on the body, for toning up the bone marrow, for sharpening the mind, for strengthening the blood and heart, and as a potent yang sexual tonic intended solely for men. Deer antlers contain strong hormones which interact with certain male hormones to produce heightened sexual activity, it is said. Take up to four capsules one hour before retiring to bed with your wife or mate.

QUAN YIN FORMULAS I & II: Designed especially for women. Formula I is for PMS and painfully, difficult menstruation. Among the ingredients are red raspberry leaves, the roots of golden seal, peony, and ginger, squaw vine, and cramp bark. Take one to three capsules daily with meals as needed. Formula II is for women entering or passing through menopause. Among the ingredients are the roots of bupleurum, Chinese foxglove, peony, ginger, and acathopanax. Take one to two capsules daily with meals.

QUAN YIN FORMULAS III (TIGRESS) and IV (TIGER): Formula III is designed for the energy needs of today's active-minded women and also contains the roots of astragalus, Chinese foxglove, peony, Chinese licorice, and ginger, powdered cayenne pepper. Recommended intake is two capsules daily with meals; double that amount for hectic schedules or physically demanding tasks. Formula IV is intended for active men and contains ginseng, astragalus, stag horn, royal jelly, foo-ti-teng, sarsaparilla, damiana, gotu kola, and cayenne. Some of these ingredients actually help strengthen masculine sexual prowess since they directly influence a man's genitalia. An average of two capsules daily is suggested, but double or even triple this amount may be necessary for ultimate bedroom performance with a spouse. Li Chung Yun used many of these same ingredients to make his two dozen wives during his 250-year lifespan extremely happy and sexually satisfied.

These are the wonderful herbal creations of the greatest living Chinese health legend, Dr. Li Chung Yun. They are available only from Albi Imports (see Appendix for a repeat of the address and phone number). If unavailable in your area have your local health food retailer contact ALBI IMPORTS to get them in for you:

19029 36th Ave. West
Unit B
Linnwood, WA. 98036
(206)-778-9494

7188 Curragh Av.
Burnaby, B.C.
Canada V5J 4V9
(604)-438-1054

CHAPTER SIX

AN ENVIROMENTAL RELIGION:
HOW THE AMAZON TRIBES WORSHIP

Rethinking Judeo-Christian Concepts

Inherent within the tenets of Judaism and Christianity is the basic belief in the Fatherhood of God. Scriptures are abundantly clear in the writings of both religions that either God is the Father of the human race or else this and the fact that Jesus Christ was His Only Begotten Son. Here again the implication is being made that God actually sired a Son, both in the spirit as well as in the flesh. But in the midst of all of this, we usually never hear any references made to God's female counterpart. If a holy and resurrected divine being like Himself is to be the Father of All Living, then common-sense dictates that He surely needs to have a wife to round out this heavenly parental role. For while a He might sire spirits, a She is definitely required to bear all of those wonderful spirit sons and daughters. In all of this divine scheme, then, where does our Heavenly Mother figure in?

The *Talmud* and the Holy *Bible* also speak of an undefined region called Heaven or Paradise in rather nebulous terms. Here go all good and righteous spirits to live happily ever after, while naughty ones go to another, unspecified locale known only as Hell or Hades. But just where are such places? Do they, in fact, exist right here on earth but in a different dimension of time and matter? Or do we look elsewhere, beyond planet earth, somewhere deeper in outer space?

And what about the houses we live in, the places we work at, the parks we play in, the mountains we camp in or ski on, the rivers we fish or the oceans we swim in and sail and surf upon? Are they entirely devoid of unseen hosts, and are we the only really intelligent beings there? Or, perhaps, might there be invisible spirits in all of these places, both friendly as well as unfriendly, that influence our lives for good or bad?

Such are some of the important theological aspects considered in this chapter. But surprisingly enough, they originate with so-called "heathen" Indian nations in South America, rather than with Jews and Christians. Learning more about them will help each one of us to cultivate a greater reverence and respect for motherhood in general, the spirit world in particular, and nature overall.

Our Mother in Heaven

One of the most fundamental doctrines inherent to the beliefs of most tropical forest tribes in South America was the existence of a heavenly mother or female goddess counterpart to the more familiar masculine role of a Supreme Being. Overlooked in the Islamic and Judeo-Christian religion, this important concept placed women on a nearly equal footing with men in the eternal affairs of governing. Only the Mormon religion emphasizes a similar theme, while the rest of Catholic and Protestant Christianity still pretty much adhere to the old notion of an all-male Deity.

Commonsense tells us that if women share with men the burdens of this world, especially the joys and sorrows of child-bearing and rearing, then why shouldn't they share in the same rewards of happiness and glory Hereafter? Not even North American Indian tribes went this far, although many of them did assign a feminine gender to such things as the earth and corn. Ruth M. Underhill mentioned in her book, *Red Man's America* (Chicago, 1973), that the Pueblo Indians began their version of the Book of Genesis with Mother Earth and Father Sky. But while the Pawnee and Osage tribes may have made frequent mention of their Mother Corn, they always spoke to the male star in the heavens or to a very masculine sun deity. Even the ultimate power—the Great Spirit—was always referred to in the masculine genders of He or Him, but never She or Her. It is only in the religions of the Amazon jungle tribes that we begin to find frequent mention made of a divine creator or goddess actually sharing supernatural responsibilities and power with her husband.

Furthermore, the family unit becomes more extended with the inclusion of twin sons, which sometimes turn out to be either very good or very evil. Their births are attributed to some kind of sexual union between the chief god and goddess. The closest parallel one can find in all of Christianity is the Mormon idea that Jesus and Lucifer were the first-and second-born sons of a Heavenly Father and a Heavenly Mother. Hence, among tropical forest tribes the family unit was held especially sacred because of such noble and interesting beliefs.

Consider, for instance, the two greatest personages of Apapocuva Guarani mythology—a culture which flourished extensively at one time in Paraguay and southern Brazil. The most majestic deity of all was the Creator or Nanderuvucu, also known as the Great Father. His wife was no less important than he was. Referred to as the first woman, Nandecy or the lovely Mother, she lived in the west in the Land-Without-Evil.

The Mundurucu were once a Tupi-speaking people residing in the southwestern part of the State of Para and the southeastern corner of the State of Amazonas, Brazil. Their creator god and big culture hero was Karusakaibo (also spelled Karusakaibe or Karusakeibu). The woman who shared his throne was once an ordinary Mundurucu whom he took to Heaven and married. Her name was Sikrida and she bore him an eldest son (Korumtau) and a younger one (Anukeite or Hanu-Acuate). In some of the old Mundurucu legends, the business of creation and populating this world involved all four of them. In other words, woman was able to contribute significantly to the formation of this planet and the beings who have inhabited it.

Claude Levi-Strauss reported that some of the lesser known tribes which once inhabited the right bank of the Guapore River in western Brazil, worshipped a married couple who had divine offspring. The Amniapa and Guarataga, in particular, attributed the creation of the world to Arikagnon, who married Panannakoza, and then fathered the beat culture heroes, Arikepua and Konanopo (the instructor of farming).

Alfred Metraux mentioned that the tribes of the Jurua-Purus River basins in the southwestern lowlands of the Brazilian Province of Amazonas, entertained corresponding beliefs. The Cashinawa, for instance, believed.in an Old Father (or Poke, The Good One), who lived in the sky with his wife, the Old Mother. Both ruled the so called Lightning People. Their main function together was to carry to heaven the souls of the dead and to provide them with all kinds of foods and gods. However, he and his good wife expected them to work and be diligent. Whenever thunder occurred, they imagined it to be the tears of the old man and woman, sobbing when they thought of their lost children.

In this simple but beautiful tale, we can find evidence of joint cooperation between husband and wife deities, who seem to care very much for their children on earth, even to the point of shedding tears. A similar parallel occurs in one of the canonized scriptures of the Mormon Church, called *The Pearl of Great Price*. In the book of Moses 7:28, Enoch is surprised to find the God of Heaven weeping buckets of tears when shown a grand and glorious vision of the universe. He inquires why God is crying so much? The answer comes back because these acts are the workmanship of my own hands, but due to their great wickedness and refusal to repent, he would end up having to destroy them.

In both accounts, the deified male comes across as an extremely compassionate, tender-hearted, and long-suffering soul, capable of the same emotions that a mother might feel when something has happened to one of her children. He also assumes his share of the parenting responsibilities (in this case, conducting dead souls to Heaven) along with his good wife. This nurturing role for a masculine in company with a female goddess, presents a much more realistic picture of things as they could be, or ought to be, in eternity. It also makes worshipping a lot easier for women, knowing that they have a female counterpart somewhere up there with whom they can share their innermost thoughts and desires. Knowledge of such a thing would seem to be far more comforting to a woman than knowing that the only deity she prayed to was a masculine being incapable of understanding how she felt as a woman! Clearly, the forest tribes of the Amazon, however primitive and backward they might have been in other things, certainly were well ahead of us in defining their deities.

The first and most logical step in formulating a new environmental religion for yourself, is to think in terms of a married couple instead of just men calling all the shots in eternity. And to believe in the idea that *there is a woman in Heaven*, sharing in the business of creating worlds, people, animals and other things in conjunction with her husband. To say that it's a 50-50 split may be carrying things a little far, but certainly to expect her *significant* input into what happens, both there and here, is not only realistic but very, very possible!

Voyages of the Soul

Among the unusual concepts currently promulgated within the New Age movement, one of the more fascinating and popular ones has been astral projection, wherein the spirit can leave its body at random and travel just about anywhere it wants. Such a thing, of course, is regarded as being from the Evil One by conservative Christians and was never found among Native American beliefs.

However, some of the forest tribes in the Amazon tropics did believe that the soul could take nightly sojourns into different realms of experience through the simple medium of dreams. The Tarirape, for instance, who once inhabited central Brazil just west of the Araguya River and north of the Tapirape River, believed that dreams were like voyages, when the soul gets free of the body and travels through space and time. During these frequent trips, the soul might travel to regions which are not known to the living, and are inhabited by spirits. Here the soul could learn and experience things which it might never be able to do in the awakened flesh. Also, such expeditions of the soul into the spiritual realm, while the body slumbered, often gave it greater power over mischievous imps and spirits.

In north central Brazil, about where the Amazon empties into the Atlantic Ocean is also where the Xingu River starts its southward course. Some miles down, one of its smaller branches becomes the Batovi River. Along here once dwelled the Bacairi Indians (four villages containing about 700 people in 1884). This particular tribe had a matrilineal government: the mothers and their respective descendants in each family presided over the affairs of every nuclear unit. Among all of the tribes of the Upper Xingu, only the Becairi women seem to have enjoyed a special status with their men—they were allowed to participate in most of the religious feasts and rituals, from which women were of the other tribes were completely excluded. Furthermore, the women had their own exclusively feminine festivals, which their men weren't allow to take part in.

Buell Ouain, an ethnologist who spent some time among these Indians in the late 1890s, reported that these people believed that a man required a woman in order for his soul to drift temporarily from his body while it slept and roam around wherever it pleased. Those not fortunate enough to have good women by their sides, either in a matrimonial sense or just living together, usually had many bad dreams portending ill events, which often signified an imprisonment of their souls in their sleeping bodies.

The Bacairi believed that everyone had not one but two souls and clearly drew distinctions between them. The "cover" portion of the soul was what could freely travel around each night during slumber. But the "ghost" part continued to remain inside the body until one day released by death. Then it underwent consecutive metamorphoses, becoming first a wandering soul (often in the shape of an armadillo), and later it became liberated, and climbed to the sky on a cotton ladder and joined its ancestors in its final state called "yamdra."

It was this outer layer or "cover" of the soul, however, which took frequent nightly voyages above, beneath, and upon the earth. When it returned again to the body and became reunited with its other "ghost" half prior to reawakening at dawn, it brought with it much valuable information which the "ghost" portion could later process in the mortal mind.

An illustration of just how this thing might work in reference to dreams can be found in the apocryphal *Book of Jasher* (Salt lake City, 1888) 48:1-6, describing the time that Joseph was a prisoner in Egypt:

"At that time Pharoah king of Egypt was sitting upon his throne in the land of Egypt, and lay in his bed and dreamed dreams, and Pharoah saw in his dream that he was standing by the side of the river of Egypt. And whilst he was standing he saw and behold seven fat fleshed and well favored kine came up out of the river.

"And seven other kine, lean fleshed and ill favored, came up after them, and the seven ill favored ones swallowed up the well favored ones, and still their appearance was ill as at first. And he awoke, and he slept again and he dreamed a second time...and [then] Pharoah awoke out of his dream.

"And in the morning the king remembered his dreams, and his spirit was sadly troubled on account of his dreams..."

Here we have some idea of the unique Bacairi belief in action. Pharoah's "cover" apparently went into the spirit world dimension, which stood parallel to the physical world of Egypt then as now, and witnessed these fat and lean cattle. When it rejoined it's other half, it conveyed these scenes of despair. Upon the body's reawakening, the "ghost" or spirit part of the soul become "sadly troubled."

In a time when astral projections are the rage and favor of some New Age adherents, it becomes much more practical to seriously regard the sensibleness of this particular Bacalri belief. It is not only worthy of our deepest attention but also our utmost desire. For, unlike what the former offers, this only teleports the intellectual part—the cover—of the soul, not its fluid or ghostly portion which needs to remain inside the body until death finally separates it from the flesh.

Although no specific information on exactly how this was accomplished by the Bacalri Indians was recorded, suffice it to say that normal midnight dreams were the means by which such adventuresome jaunts could be made. And, more importantly, for some unexplained reason, women were an integral key to more fulfilling and meaningful trips for the "covers" of men's souls.

Next on the agenda, it would seem, in developing a new religion for yourself in the turbulent and uncertain nineties, would be petitioning your Heavenly Parents for great dreams and nightly sojourns filled with purpose and discovery. As we've shown before, many of the Amazon forest tribes worshipped male and female deities together instead of just one or the other. Most orthodox Christians and Jews today address only God the Man in masculine terms, while at the opposite end of the pendulum swing are liberated women who pray only to She or Her. An amalgamation of both, as once practiced by the Amazon Indians, appears to offer a much more balanced and sensible approach to things for those seeking new kinds of enlightenment and better ways of worshipping what they conceive Deity to be.

Dreaming is a gift granted to us by the grace of our Heavenly Parents. And if the Bacairi were correct in their notion that it takes a good woman to make beautiful dreams, then couldn't we assume a similar thing for the goddess who reigns beside her godly husband in power and glory?

Respect For Life and the Hereafter

Judeo-Christian beliefs have failed to adequately address the importance of treating our animals well and taking proper care of our environment. Consequently, many otherwise decent and devoted souls do not understand that these issues are of paramount significance so far as eternal salvation goes. Perhaps one thing which contributes to a lack of sufficient understanding in these matters is the prevailing attitude among many devout believers that animal and plant life are somehow less important than human life. Another notion probably is that the way we behave towards such life forms really doesn't affect our ultimate salvation much. In either case, nothing could be further from the truth!

The tropical forest Indians of the dense Amazon jungles had much to contribute in this regard, and from them we can certainly learn a lot to set our thinking straight on these issues. It was their firm belief that the way someone treated an animal or took care of the environment determined quite a bit just how much they advanced in the next world. Treat other life forms with dignity and respect and you could count on being in a very nice paradise of some sort; but abuse them in any way and you could expect taking up permanent residency in a spirit world or worse Hereafter!

The Barama Carib of the Rio Negro in northern Brazil believed in bush spirits who controlled different parts of the surrounding environment. They recognized five distinct categories with a controlling master in each, the classes being associated, respectively, with the forest and land generally; the air; the water; the hills; and miscellaneous places or things, such as houses and industries. These various spirit masters had to report to higher spirit authorities regarding the attitude and treatment of mortals to each of these separate environments.

If someone was guilty of burning more of the forest away than was necessary for cultivation, that would be reported and judged to be a sin. Or if the air was fouled by too much smoke, it would be considered a rash act. Or if the water was polluted without any reason, those responsible were held in condemnation. Later in the Hereafter, such a one who burned the trees could possibly expect to find himself in a barren desert; or they who polluted the air or water, residing inside an active volcano or near a filthy swamp.

Consider, for instance, what the fate could be (by Barama Carib standards) of the owner in Hagersville, Canada (just 60 miles south of Toronto), who neglected to adequately protect his 14 million used tires from burning out of control through much of 1990. The nearly 2,000 degrees inferno generated 100,000 gallons of runoff oil in less than ten days. It also contaminated the ground water in some neighboring wells and poured huge billows of black smoke laced with deadly benzenes and dioxins into the atmosphere. Perhaps such a fellow might find himself someday in a nether part of the spirit world constantly exposed to burning coal and tar as a fitting punishment for the environmental sins he committed while still in mortality. At least that's what the Barama Carib imagined happened, and it should put us on better notice as to how we take care of the environment, lest we should find ourselves dwelling in unpleasant areas of the spirit world.

The Taulipang Indians of the northern Amazon regions believed that even trees, plants, animals, birds, and fish possessed souls and reasoning intellects of some kind. When they were mistreated or abused by men, they could effectively bar a person's advancement into a higher glory or paradise Hereafter. Consider, for instance, what they claimed befell a master who mistreated his dog. The man's soul, upon death, would ascend to the sky and from there proceed on to the Milky Way, which was the Taulipang equivalent of our Heaven. But an assortment of animals guarded the way. If an owner had abused his pet on earth, then the dog was very likely to tear his soul to shreds before he ever reached his final destination.

The Tenetehara once inhabited the Amazon region drained by the Mearim, Grajau and Pindare Rivers in the state of Maranhao. This region was originally a very dense tropical rain forest rich in hardwoods, rubber, copaiba, and various palms, whose leaves and nuts were important to their economic life. Among their pantheon of gods was Maranauwa, Lord of all the surrounding forest and of the animals inhabiting them. They believed that he punished all Tenetehara men who needlessly and wantonly kill the white-lipped peccaries and other game. Other Tupi groups identified him as Corropira or Kuri-pira, who could inflict terrible misery on reckless hunters and fishermen if he chose to.

Of course, to most of us in a more enlightened era, such things strike us more as quaint and curious folklore instead of the serious truths they really are. Not that dogs tear souls to shreds, nor forest gods give us hell Hereafter, but that *we are severely judged* in the next world on how we treated animals here!

In the northern part of South America lay the Guianas. They are bounded coastally by the Atlantic to the east and north, their northern interior boundary is the right bank of the Orinoco River, where, from the mouth of the Apure River to the ocean, its course takes a general east-to west direction. The southern boundary is the left bank of the Amazon River from its confluence with the Rio

Negro to its northernmost mouth. The western boundaries of the Guianas, for practical purposes, may be said to include the right bank of the Orinoco River, upstream from its meeting with the Apure River to its head; an arbitrary straight line from the head of the Orinoco southeastward to the mouth of the Catrimani River (a right tributary of the Rio Branco); the left bank of the Rio Branco southward to its confluence with the Rio Negro; and the left bank of the Rio Negro southeastward to its final meeting point with the mighty Amazon itself.

Encompassing this huge geographical region, are four very different kinds of environment: coastal plains and deltas which are low, often swampy, subject to periodic flooding, and covered with thick swamp forest growth; higher inland forests which are more pervasive and abundant; savanna grasslands occasionally dotted with drought-resistant trees and undergrowth; and finally, very mountainous rain forest terrain within the interior regions, containing many spectacular waterways and numerous smaller streams abounding in fish of every kind.

In the first quarter of this century, there were ten major aboriginal linguistic families inhabiting these then-uncivilized environs: Arawakan, Awaken, Cariban, Calianan, Macuan, Muran, Salivan (or Macuan), Shirianan, Tupian, and the Warruan or Guaraunan. Since prehistoric times, these many different families of separate tribes have intermingled with one another in trade, marriage, and warfare. As a result, a great deal of cultural intermixing has occurred over many centuries, leaving just a few distinct traits identifiable within each group.

According to ethnologist John Gillin, the cosmogony of the known tribes in this area follows certain patterns. For one thing, they all believe in a head honcho deity or boss spirit (as Cillian calls it).

This boss spirit gathered around himself, in the beginning of time, a certain number of other lesser but highly important spirits, some of whom were men and others of whom were animals. Both classes of spirits figured heavily in the creation of people and animals in general. For instance, among the Caribs, the bunia bird was frequently credited with teaching the Indians how to use cultivated plants and other culture traits, because of its involvement in their original spiritual creations. As another example of this unique belief, the boss spirit assigned jaguars the task of having a more powerful influence over men.

This helps to explain why forest tribe shamans underwent a lengthy preparation to become intimately familiar with these assorted spirits—man, bird, beast, or reptile. It is interesting to note that women played an important role in these spiritual initiations

—young maidens for their beauty and purity and older ones for their strength and wisdom.

A number of candidates are initiated in a special house by a medicine man, assisted by an old woman and a virgin for each candidate. The course lasts 24 days and nights, and involves different ordeals, such as drinking tobacco water, putting pepper in the eyes, and dancing without sleep.

Now before the reader is tempted to consign all of these beliefs to harmless mythology, it may be well to remember this: near similar corresponding truths may be found in present-day Christian writings. I'm referring to no less of an authority than the King James' *Bible*! The entire fourth chapter of Revelation of St. John the Divine," refers to a "boss spirit" surrounded by several unusual creatures and two dozen men, all of whom appeared to be advising, worshipping, and praising Him *in unison*!

"I looked, and, behold, a door was opened in heaven. Behold, a throne was set in heaven, and one sat on the throne... And round about the throne were four and twenty seats: and upon the seats I saw four and twenty elders... And round about the throne were four beasts... The first beast was like a lion, the second beast was like a calf, the third beast had a face as a man, and the fourth beast was like a flying eagle... And they rest not day and night, saying, Holy, holy, holy, Lord God Almighty... And when those beasts give glory and honour and thanks to him that sat on the throne...the four and twenty elders fall down before...and worship him"

Our third logical step, then, in formulating a new religion for ourselves in the nineties and beyond seems to be this: Beyond recognizing a married couple as ruling deity and the medium of dreams through which part of the soul can travel during our nightly slumbers, should come an undeniable admission that animals play a more significant role in both our creation and eventual judgment than we have heretofore realized.

Consequently, it's dependent upon every one of us to treat all living creatures better than we have done, and never to use their flesh or fur or feathers for anything, other than what might be necessary for our food, clothing, or shelter. We must never beat them, nor imprison them, nor work them unnecessarily, nor abandon them, nor inflict upon them painful surgical procedures (in the form of neutering or "fixing") so they could never again give birth. If we are guilty of any of the above at any time in our lives, then surely repentance is in order, lest any of them stand beside us at the Judgment Bar of God someday and bring railing accusations of cruelty and carelessness against us.

Also as part of our new religion for the rest of this decade and the next century should come more of an inculcated respect for the environment. For, as the tropical forest Indians of South America correctly believed, there are spirits or invisible guardians of the air, mountains, hills, valleys, meadows, rivers, lakes, and oceans around us. If we pollute or befoul any of them, whether by throwing an empty beer can or Kleenex tissue out of the window or carelessly flipping a smoked cigarette into dry underbrush, then we are guilty of some form of environmental abuse, no matter how small the act of negligence may have been. Again, if we do not reform our ways and repent of these particular transgressions, then surely we will have a lot of explaining to do come Judgment Day, which could prove to be both extremely embarrassing and terribly unpleasant!

Life after Death

Our final consideration in devising a more workable belief system for the rest of this decade has to do with that society in the next world to which individual spirits go once they've laid their bodies into the grave. Unlike the reports which have come back from many of those who've had "near death experiences" and claimed that their trips were pleasant and peaceful, most of the tropical forest tribes imagined such a journey for the soul as fraught with risks and dangers.

Consider the Paressi Indians who once occupied the Mato Grosso region of central Brazil for many years. The souls of their departed loved ones were believed to travel to the sky, but on the way they had to cope with a number of difficult ordeals. For instance, they were made to pass by a large bonfire which burned the 'sinners' and by a doglike monster which tore at them if they had been unkind to animals. If, however, they succeeded in overcoming these dangers, the souls were received in the sky by a deity known as Waikomone and his three brothers, who honored them as brave warriors and noble maidens.

The Manasi of eastern Bolivia and the Madeira headwaters, had an even more interesting and rather complete set of beliefs regarding what happened Hereafter. To begin with, all souls were judged by a holy male trinity of three gods and one chief female goddess. The head honcho was (O)mequituriqui or God Father, who with his goddess Ouipozi, procreated the Urasana or God Son. This family trio, in turn, was closely associated with Urapo Stiquitetu, the Thunder Cod.

The God Father, they believed, spoke in a high-pitched voice and was like a judge and avenger of the people. Diseases and deaths were attributed to him and he used these means to scourge and humble his people. But Urasana, the God Son, his Heavenly Mother the goddess Quipozi interceded for mankind and stayed many of the chief god's terrible judgments against humanity.

What is so nice about this particular belief and makes a lot of sense here is that woman figures heavily in the factor of saving grace, along with the more traditional God Son. In basic Judeo-Christian beliefs this concept is wholly lacking, with just divine men alone being capable of showing compassion and mercy. But as ethnologist Alfred Metraux correctly noted:

The goddess Cuipozi enjoyed much popularity. She was ordinarily addressed as the Mother, and was visualized as a large woman, dressed in a white garment, who protected people from being harmed by the other gods.

It is even more fascinating to see that in their belief system, she shared a nearly equal role with the other gods when they communed with their favorite tribal shamans. Sanctuaries called pooriri (which were nothing more than extremely large huts) served as the temples into which the shamans would to carry on a long conversation [with] the gods about future events, such as seasonable rains, bountiful harvests, successful hunting and fishing expeditions, and the issue of prospective war raids. These interviews were carried on by him in a loud voice.

All of this is quite noteworthy, especially when one realizes that the Manasi, like so many other jungle tribes of their day, had an exclusive male priesthood into which no village women were ever admitted. In their religion, however, one woman at least (Cuipozi), held high status and almost equal ranking with other important gods.

Furthermore this goddess Cuipozi would sometimes assist those who had died of illnesses to the land of the Dead. Occasionally, the sick person might invoke her to come to his bedside, where she would commence upbraiding the other gods for afflicting him in the manner they had done. She would stay beside him for a while, acting as a kind of immortal Florence Nightingale, taking care of his needs and wants and speaking soothing words to his distressed mind and troubled heart. If her sharp criticism didn't turn the gods away from their punishment of this poor fellow, then she would tarry with his departed soul on the lone and arduous journey to the Manasi version of paradise—an pleasant country abounding with honey, fish, and certain large trees that exuded a resin. Here we can see that woman again played a vital role in the salvation of quite a few Manasi souls.

Once the Manasi soul had reached the land of the Dead, it would then be ushered into one of several regions. Where each soul went was determined by the place where they had died. Each category of souls had a different name. The Asinecca had perished near a river and had gone to the land of the water gods (Ysituuca), which teemed with fish, bananas, and parrots. The Yirituuca had died in the bush, and the Posirabca had died in their own homes.

As Metraux observed in the *Handbook of South American Indians*, the Manao (an Arawakan tribe of the left, middle Amazon, residing below the Rio Negro and lower Ica Rivers) believed in two gods—one benevolent and kind (Mauari) and the other very evil (Saraua), who both emanated from the same goddess. Furthermore, the upper world to which righteous souls eventually went, was divided into several layers presided over by Mauari, while bad people went down to a nether world ruled by Saraua. According to Metraux, the Mojo tribe, which once inhabited that jungle region in eastern Bolivia bordered by the Mamore, Guapay, and Yacuma Rivers, believed that this nether world was located right here on earth, but in another dimension of time, and that many departed spirits hung around the haunts and habitations they once occupied in mortal life. The Siriono (Mbia), also of the high forested areas in eastern and northern Bolivia, thought that after death, people can become evil spirits and be able to harm mortals, if they wish to.

Qualifying for entrance into the tribal equivalent of paradise, depending on several things. For instance, your behavior and moral conduct on earth had a lot to do with where you might end up in the Hereafter. Tribes along the eastern slopes of the Bolivian Andes believed that this pleasant heaven was open only to those who never violated traditional customs. This included treating your fellow human beings right, conducting yourself according to the moral code of your respective tribe (no adultery, for instance), and giving plenty of offerings to the gods and goddesses.

Also, only children or those with childlike spirits to them, could get to paradise without a lot of difficulty. One of the Guarani tribes of Paraguay and southern Brazil, the Apapocuva, believed that only children's souls can easily reach the Land-Without-Evil. Also those adults who had inherited childlike traits such as meekness and humility, could usually go straight to this paradise.

Some tropical forest tribes also believed in a type of guardian spirit or angel for each mortal. The notorious Jivaro head-hunters in the Montana of Ecuador just north of the Maranon River, held to the view that particular guardian spirits called old ones, protected tribal members from bad spirits and other unseen evil influences most of the time. The Cashinawa, of the Tupian family which roamed the Jurua-Purus lowland basins in the southwestern portion of the Brazilian Province of Amazonas, felt that when a man died, his soul was taken to the sky by a spirit. There it 'woke up again' and lived forever with the 'Great Ancestor' in a pleasant country with no evil or suffering. A number of tribes believed that every mortal was blessed with some type of helpful guardian; some even went so far as to suggest masculine spirits for men and feminine spirits for women.

Another consideration entertained by some Amazon natives was an undefined omnipresent power of some sort. Claude Levi-Strauss observed that Indians in the Guapore River region seem to believe in the existence of an invisible fluid which may be good or evil. By various gesticulations the shaman captures and manipulates it into food, into the sick, or into the bodies of enemies. Levi-Strauss also mentioned that the Nambicuara Indians, living in a large area northwest of the Guapore River, likewise, believe in the existence of a broad power or material which may occur in objects and in living beings.

Collectively speaking, some of the tropical forest tribes held to the notion that there was a *higher* power or substance *above* all the various gods and goddesses, including the boss god himself. This unseen force not only sustained every living thing on earth, but also in the universe. In fact, it was what made deities more powerful, turning ordinary men and women into supernatural heroes and heroines. Conversely, though, this same invisible power could also become an evil force to be reckoned with, if put into and handled by spirits, gods, or goddesses who were malevolent in their natures and behaviors.

By this same power, good shamans could work acts of mercy on behalf of the needy, while bad witches and wizards could stir up some pretty potent trouble if they so desired. The invisible substance itself, however, remained relatively neutral and without any kind of emotions, until some of it was handled by righteous mortals and deities, improperly used for wicked purposes by bad men and spirits. Then, and only then, could it either progress or retrogress with the good or bad feelings acquired from those who happen to be using some of it.

One 19th century scholar familiar with some of the ancient religious beliefs of Amazonian Indians, referred to it as The Great First Cause or that intelligent force which was before anything else ever was. By it and through it, South American tribes believed, everything and everyone came into being, whether for good or for evil intents. When a person died and went into the next life, he or she took with them whatever portion of this power that they might have accumulated in mortality. Thus, it was to a person's advantage to acquire as much of this invisible substance for good as possible while still in the flesh, so as to give him or her a more definite edge on things in the Hereafter.

A New Way of Worshipping

The idea for a new set of revised religious concepts centered around the environment first occurred to me during a 1979 trip I made with other scientists to the Soviet Union. In the Black Sea resort metropolis of Sukhumi, I met a Russian divorcee in her early 40's named Ludmila Melnikova. She spoke near-perfect English and we had a glorious six-hour visit together with her two teenage daughters, Irina (then 17) and Alla (then 16) in a city park.

Having been raised in an atheistic culture, she knew nothing about the Holy Trinity, much less of Heaven or Hell. But through the years she had gradually formulated some ideas of her own relative to religion. I distinctly remember her telling me in her slightly accented English that she worshipped "the God of Nature," whom she conceived to be both divine matter and divine deity. She felt very strongly that a feminine spirit also was quite pervasive in the creation process, but didn't know exactly just how far-reaching it was. Nor did she know for sure if there was a "Goddess of Nature," but agreed with the notion I advanced that there could be a mother in Heaven or mother deity somewhere, besides her already accepted male figure.

While addressing this "God of Nature," she insisted that she *never* imagined herself praying to the sky or the trees or the grass or the rocks or the animals or the birds, but rather to a distinct intelligence, which she felt at times "almost had to be a person, it seems." She indicated to me that, were she to fully embrace my idea of a Heavenly Mother, she seriously doubted whether she would address her in any prayers as Goddess of Nature." She laughed good-heartedly and replied that she felt quite comfortable opening her frequent petitions with "O God of Nature," but would probably start thinking in terms of a female partner for Him from now on.

Ludmila didn't hesitate to tell me that this unique concept of a Mother Deity helped, to explain to her satisfaction at least, how so many spirits might have been created long ago, through a birthing process similar to that responsible for bringing children into this world, but probably of a much shorter time span.

Her own opinions regarding the "life force" (as she called it) in each of us, was a bit vague. She had never completely decided whether it was without shape or, in fact, possessed distinct features not unlike those representing her real body. But when pressed a little for clearer details, she humorously admitted that there was something which left the body at death and went somewhere else, but exactly where she knew not. However, she had never heard of anything like astral projections, commenting that something so strange as this could, perhaps, be a bit dangerous. Nor was she familiar with any of the South American Indian beliefs regarding dreams as the medium by which a part of the soul could freely wander during slumber, which I was just beginning to research at the time. But, in a half whimsical, half teasing fashion, I recall her adding something to the effect that it probably wouldn't hurt to ask her "God of Nature" to give her some better dreams hereafter so she could rest well.

However, on the point of injuring the environment or needlessly hurting animals, she was in full accord with the views held by the Amazon tribes. This concerned not so much individual spirits controlling this or that in nature, but rather with their idea that purposely harming things brought great displeasure, if not downright anger and retribution, from that God Himself! She envisioned acts of negligence ranging from carelessly walking across a beautiful flower bed to the thoughtless killing of a Siberian silver fox for his costly fur, as the equivalents of spitting in or slapping the face of her "God of Nature" (assuming, of course, that he was in the form of a man).

"Whenever I pray," she said in rather good English, "I always try to remind myself to ask my 'God of Nature' to help me be a better protector of his beauty around me and to not behave shamefully towards it at any time." By doing this often, she reasoned, it would probably help her to get wherever she was going in the next existence. She knew nothing, though, about animals having a possible influence in the creation process and frankly discounted such as "innocent mythology."

This former English teacher, who once held a position of distinction at Moscow University but had of late been reduced to doing custodial chores, was an extremely intelligent and very articulate woman who had managed to form a simple creed that embodied a great deal of childlike faith. While it obviously didn't contain all of the answers she needed, it had carried Ludmila and her teenage daughters through some very rough and trying times, giving the small family strength to remain intact when outside forces threatened to split them apart.

This lengthy interview took place while Leonid Brezhnev was still in power and the era of Gorbachev's glasnost had not yet dawned. Religious oppression still existed, with the exception of the Russian Orthodox Church, which was the only recognized religion permitted to flourish in those days. One wonders, however, since the recent influx of considerable religious liberty, whether or not Ludmila would have been able to continue in her simple beliefs without seeing them corrupted by an onslaught of Protestant doctrines that demean women and have very little regard for the environment.

For those in search of something better, this chapter has offered a variety of religious ideas, borrowed from the cultures of the South American Amazon jungle, which make sense and are more meaningful than much of the material currently being presented by both the New Age movement and traditional Christianity. It contains the basic elements of a faith in a god and goddess who care very much for their children here. Likewise, it suggests the premortal birth of deified twin brothers—one who becomes very good and holy, and the other who eventually turns out to be very bad and ill-tempered. Furthermore, this chapter addresses the subject of the soul in man and beast alike, a part of which can probably drift at random during periods of slumber. We find herein that animals have significant status in the next world, too. Those intending to get to a pleasant paradise after death had better treat their pets and the surrounding environment a lot better than they've heretofore done.

Admittedly, the all-important issue of Biblical Redeemer in the form of Christ is the central point of present-day Christianity; for without such a Saviour figure as Jesus, the faith of millions of loyal disciples would undoubtedly wither away in no time at all. Yet did He not encourage His own followers to do works similar to what they had seen Him do, if they loved Him dearly? He always spoke of a personal Father, regularly communed with a Holy Spirit, treated women with dignity and respect, and was kind to men and beasts alike. Essentially then, these are the same elements of faith and behavior by which Amazon tribes worshipped and conducted themselves. Yet they had no personal concept of a resurrected Lord as Christians have today. But in the final analysis of things, they appear to have been ultimately saved by the warm and wonderful graces extended to them by loving Heavenly Parents in whom the Fatherhood of Man and the Motherhood of Woman have become equally fulfilled and realized!

CHAPTER SEVEN

A SENECA PROPHET SPEAKS TO AMERICA: CODE OF HANDSOME LAKE

A Native American Prophet

Handsome Lake, the Seneca prophet whose remarkable teachings comprise this final chapter, was born in 1735 in the Seneca village of Conawagas on the Genesee River opposite the present town of Avon, Livingston Co., N.Y. He was described by one Iroquois, Buffalo Tom Jemison, as a middle-aged man, slim and unhealthy looking. He was a member of one of the noble families in which the title of Canio'dai'io' or Ska'niadar'io' is vested, thus holding the most honored Seneca title. What his warrior name was isn't known and neither is it known just when he received the name and title by which he later became known. It is known, however, that he belonged to the Turtle clan. Later he was "borrowed" by the Wolf clan and reared by them. His half brother was the celebrated Corn planter.

The general story of his life may be gleaned mostly from a perusal of his code of living, there being nothing of any consequence known of his life up to the time of his great vision. In 1794 his name appears on a treaty, but whether he took an active part in the debates that led up to it isn't known.

However, it is known from oral traditions and from his own story that he was a dissolute person and a miserable victim of chronic alcoholism. Losing Genesee country that formerly belonged to his people to the white man caused him to go with his tribe to the Allegheny river settlements instead. Here he became afflicted with a kind of wasting disease that was aggravated by his chronic drinking problem. From what scant information there is, one might conclude that Handsome Lake suffered from beriberi, or endemic neuritis. This disease results mainly from a thiamine deficiency in the diet, due to chronic alcoholism or self-imposed starvation or uncontrolled famine. It affects the sensory nerves more than the motor nerves, with symptoms commencing in the feet and working upward to the hands which are the last to be affected.

For four years he lay a helpless invalid because of this presumed condition. His bare cabin afforded him much time for serious meditation, and it is quite possible that some of his precepts are the result of much meditation and pondering during this period, besides what he learned in his remarkable vision. His own sad state deeply impressed upon him the folly of using liquor. In the foreword of his grand revelation, he tells how he became as one who was dead and of the glorious visitation of the "four [divine] beings" who appeared to him in all of their heavenly splendor and revealed the will of the Creator unto him.

After this first revelation, he seemed to make a remarkably quick recovery and immediately began to tell the story of his visions to all who were willing to listen. His initial role as a temperance reformer among his people met with instant success, but more from religious instinct than from appealing to reason. For a century, he ravages of intemperance had already made serious inroads on the domestic and social life of his people. It had demoralized their national life and caused his brother chiefs to barter their lands for the means of a debauchery. Alcohol was threatening the social and physical extinction of his people. Such were the background scenarios which served as a prelude to his great revelation. Had it not been for the visit of these four men from the Celestial World where Almighty God dwells in brilliant fire and blinding light like unto the sun itself, the entire Seneca nation would have passed into total oblivion well before the end of the 19th century.

Here was a man well past the prime of his life, a man weakened by disease and drunkenness. Yet he assumed the role of teacher and prophet. In just two years, his efforts were conducive of so much reform that they attracted the attention of U. S. President Thomas Jefferson who instructed Secretary of War Dearborn to write a letter commending the teachings of Handsome Lake. The Seneca immediately construed this as a recognition of the prophet's right to teach and prophesy. This letter came as one of the results of Handsome Lake's visit to Washington, D.C. in 1802 with a delegation of Seneca and Onondaga chiefs. The successful results of his two years' ministry became more fruitful as time went on.

True, he met with a great deal of opposition from some of the old religious diehards, who didn't want to see their traditional ways of worshipping the Great Spirit disappear. But their old Indian beliefs had virtually disappeared by the time of the Civil War, leaving just two groups of worshippers: Senecas who had converted to Christianity through the efforts of missionaries, and tribes people who had converted to the Gai'wiio' (the divinely revealed message) of their Ganiodaiio (messenger or teacher).

Arthur C. Parker, a 20th-century Iroquois chief and scholar, who wrote much about the teachings of Handsome Lake in his book,

The Code of Handsome Lake (published by New York State Museum in 1907), reported that "the success of Handsome Lake's teachings did much to crystallize the Iroquois as a distinct social group." The white man's encroaching civilization, he noted, "had demoralized the older order of things," leaving a system without any real coherent values.

Handsome Lake came at a time when the Six Nations of the Iroquois had suffered considerable fraud and defeat at the hands of the white men. They were then a beaten and dejected people, with nothing much to live for. Their tribal dignities and original self-worth had been stripped from them by the brutal and deceptive ways of white settlers and administrators. As Parker remembered it: "Poverty, the sting of defeat, the loss of ancestral homes, the memory of broken promises and the hostility of the white settlers all conspired to bring despair." In other words, they had gone so far down that there wasn't really anywhere else to go but up!

As a victim of such deplorable and tragic conditions, Handsome Lake stalked from the gloom holding up as a beacon of hope his divine message, the Gai'wiio.' He became a commanding figure, a lighted torch in the dark. He created a new system to think about, to discuss, to believe and to have hope in. His message was a creation of their own needs. It afforded a nucleus about which the Seneca could cluster, something could fasten all of their hopes upon.

Whatever may have been the merits of his teachings, they created a tremendous revolution in Iroquois religious life. With the spread of his doctrines, the older religious system still common to most Native Americans to this day, with its attendant spirit apparitions and worship of an undefined cosmic matter and thought collectively known as the Great Spirit, eventually dwindled into oblivion, being replaced by a far more sensible set of beliefs. "He was despised, ridiculed, and subjected to bodily insults," Parker recalled, but his religion lived on in the hearts of his many disciples, long after his own passing from mortality.

It wouldn't be sacrilegious to say that what Moses was to the Jews or Joseph Smith, Jr. to the Mormons, so was this man to the Iroquois Indian Confederacy. As one old Seneca tribal leader, Chief Cornplanter, described him to Parker in the early 1920s:

"He made mistakes, many mistakes...but he was only a man and men are liable to commit errors. Whatever he did and said of himself is of no consequence. What he did and said by the direction of four messengers is everything—it is our religion and nothing else! Ganiodaiio was weak in many points and sometimes afraid to do as the messengers told him. He was almost an unwilling servant in some ways. He made no divine claims, he did not pose as infallible nor even truly virtuous for that matter. He merely proclaimed the

Gai'wiio' and that is what we follow, not him. We do not worship him, we worship our great Creator. We honor and revere our prophet and leader, we revere the four messengers who watch over us—but the Creator alone do we worship and no one else!"

The highlights of Handsome Lake's brief ministry may be effectively summarized in excerpts from an important revelation which God gave to His Servant, Joseph Smith, Jr. in company with Sidney Rigdon sometime in December of 1830. It forms Section 35, verses 13-15 of the Mormon *Doctrine and Covenants* and is taken from an 1884 printed edition of the same:

"Wherefore, I call upon the weak things of the world, those who are unlearned and despised, to thrash the nations by the power of my Spirit;

"And their arm shall be my arm, and I will be their shield and their buckler; and I will gird up their loins, and they shall fight manfully for me; and their enemies shall be under their feet; and I will let fall the sword in their behalf, and by the fare of mine indignation will I preserve them.

"And the poor and the meek shall have the gospel preached unto them, and they shall be looking forth for the time of my coming, for it is nigh at hand."

This is essentially what Handsome Lake was all about: a messenger of truth, peace, and goodwill, inspired by God Above and sent unto the Seneca whom He dearly loved, with an important message especially devised for them to adhere to and live by the best way they could. His message is as timely today for white, black, and brown Americans as it still is for the Seneca and other Indians, too.

The Great Message

"Now the beings spoke saying, 'We must now relate our message. We will uncover the evil upon the earth and show how men spoil the laws the Great Ruler has made and thereby made him angry.'

"The Creator made man a living creature. Four words tell a great story of wrong and the Creator is sad because of the trouble they bring, so go and tell your people.

"The first word is One'ga' [any form of alcohol]. It seems that you never have known that this word stands for a great and monstrous evil and has reared a high mound of bones... No, the Creator did not make it for you.

"Now spoke the beings and said, We now speak of the second word. This makes the Creator angry. The word is Got'go." [The occult or metaphysical: specifically defined by them as witchcraft, seances or in today's New Age terms, channeling, tarot card and palm reading, astral projections, and so forth]. The Seneca were told that they must avoid such evils and find ways about checking the effects of such demonic things upon them, which are more applicable to the Iroquois culture. But the specific advice given to him by these four heavenly messengers to basically "let such things alone" is commonsense for rational-thinking people of all ethnic backgrounds to follow.

"Now the beings spoke again saying, This is the third word. It is a sad one, and the Creator is very sad because of this third word. It seems that you have never known that a great pile of human bodies lies dead because of this word, Ono'ityi'yende, the niga'hos'saa', the secret poisons in little bundles named Gawennodus'ha (compelling charms). Now the Creator who made us commands that they who do this evil, when they hear this message, must stop it immediately and do it nevermore while they live upon this earth-world. It matters not how much destruction they have wrought—let them repent and not fail for fear the Creator will not accept them as his own." [Parker's own footnote explanations include a variety of what we would call "good luck charms," besides the usual charms which worked spells for their owners. In this category might be included so-called lucky rabbit's foot, four-leaf clover, any Christian crucifix or small replica of a crucified Jesus, luck coin, any good-luck suit or dress].

"Now another word. It is sad. It is the fourth word. It is the way Yondwi'nias swa'yas. [Parker's footnote translation reads "she cuts it off by abortion or artificial means]."

"Now the Creator ordained that women should bear children. Now a certain young married woman had children and suffered much. Now she is with child again and her mother wishing to prevent further sufferings designs to administer a medicine to cut off the child and to prevent forever other children from coming. So the mother makes the medicine and gives it. Now when she does this she forever cuts away her daughter's string of children. [Parker observed in a bottom footnote that "the Seneca and Onondaga belief is that every woman has a certain number of children predestined to her and that they are fastened on a string-like runner like tubers, or like eggs within a bird]. Now it is because of such things that the Creator is sad. He created life to live and he wishes such evils to cease. He wishes those who employ such medicines [and operations] to cease such practices forever. Now they must stop when they hear this message. Go and tell your people [of these things]."

The messages in Sections 6 through 12 of Parker's book dealt with the marital relationships between husband and wife. Much good instruction regarding desertion, divorce, spousal abuse, and adultery/bigamy is contained therein and is very applicable to our own social ills today.

"Now another message. Go tell your people that the Great Ruler is sad because of what people do. The Creator has made it so that the married should live together and that children should grow from them.

"Now it often happens that it is only a little while when people are married that the husband speaks evil of his wife because he does not wish to care for her children. Now a man who does that stirs up trouble with his wife and soon deserts her and his children. Then he searches for another woman and when he has found her he marries her. Then when he finds her with child he goes away from her and leaves her alone. Again he looks for another woman and when he has lived with her for a time and sees her growing large, he deserts her, the third woman.

"Now this is true. We, the messengers, saw him leave the two women and the Creator himself saw him desert the third and punished him. Now a sure torment in the after life is for him who leaves two women with child but the Creator alone knows what the punishment is for the man who leaves the third.

"The Creator has ordered that man and woman should rear their children well, love them, and keep them in health. This is the Creator's rule. We, the messengers, have seen both men and women desert each other when children come. The woman discovers that the man, her husband, loves his child and she is very jealous and spreads evil reports of him. She does this for an excuse before the world to leave him. Thus the messengers say that the Creator desires men and women to cease such mischief.

"Tell your people that the Creator has ordered regular marriage customs. When the young people are old enough to marry, tell them so.

"Now another message to tell your people. The married often live well together for a while. Then a man becomes ugly in temper and abuses his wife. It seems to afford him pleasure. Now because of such things the Creator is very sad. So he bids us to tell you that such evils must stop. Neither man nor woman must strike the other... We will tell you what people must do. It is the way he calls best. Love one another and do not strive for another's undoing. Even as you desire good treatment, so render it. Treat your wife well and she will treat you well.

"This concerns both husband and wife. It may happen that a man and wife live together happily. At length the man thinks that he will go to another settlement to visit relatives there. His wife agrees and he goes. When he gets to the village he induces some agreeable woman to live with him saying he is single.

"Then after some time the man goes back to his own family. His wife treats him cordially as if no trouble had occurred. We, the messengers, say that the woman is good in the eyes of her Creator and has a place reserved for her in the heaven-world. The woman knew all that had been done in the other settlement but she thought it best to be peaceful and remain silent. And the Creator says that she is right and has her path toward the heaven-world, but, he, the man, is on his way to the house of the Wicked One."

Other messages given, which are just summarized here, include the wrongfulness of a mother-in-law to interfere with her daughter's marriage in any mischievous way and the improper disciplining of kids. "Now this is the way ordained by the Creator," observed the four messengers to Handsome Lake, for correcting youngsters: "Talk slowly and kindly to children and never punish them unjustly." Also parents were encouraged to listen to the advice sometimes offered by their kids. "When a child says, "Mother, I want you to stop wrongdoing," the child speaks straight words and the Creator says that the child speaks right and the mother must obey. Furthermore, the Creator proclaims that such words from a child are wonderful and that the mother who disregards them takes the wicked part."

The messengers declared that it was wrong for the parent to say, "I know better than you; I am the older and you are but a child; think not that you can influence me by your speaking." Observed Handsome Lake's four visitors: "Now when you tell this message to your people say that it is wrong to speak to children in such words." They also mentioned that childless couples should adopt and raise orphans as if they were their own offspring: "Moreover when a woman takes children she must rear them well as if born of herself."

The care of the elderly also occupied some of their message to Handsome Lake. "Now the Creator of mankind ordained that people should live to an old age. He appointed that when a woman becomes old she should be without strength and unable to work. [Parker's footnote indicated that "the wisdom of the aged...was never questioned" among the Seneca]. Now the Creator says that it is a great wrong to be unkind to our grandmothers. The Creator forbids unkindness to the old. We, the messengers, say it. The Creator appointed this way: he designed that an old woman should be as a child again and when she becomes so the Creator wishes the grandchildren to help her, for only because she is, they are. Whosoever does right to the aged does right in the sight of the Creator." So they said and he said, Eniaichuk.

Other instructions included: always offering food and drink to your household guests, feeding and helping the poor, stopping the spread of ill rumors and gossip, and doing away with personal boasting and vanity about one's good looks, great strength or material wealth.

"Now the Creator made food for all creatures and it must be free for all... Now when visitors enter a lodge the woman must always say, "Sede'koni'," come eat. Now it is not right to refuse what is offered. The visitor must take two or three bites at least and say, "Niawe' [thank you].".... The Creator loves poor children and whosoever feeds the poor and unfortunate does right before him. When a woman sees an unfortunate girl who has neither parents nor settled home and calls her in and helps her repair her clothing, cleanse herself, and comb her hair, she does right and has favor in the sight of her Creator. He loves the poor, and the woman does right before him."

The message given to Handsome Lake regarding the spread of gossip is worth repeating here in its entirety. While directed specifically towards women, it's just as applicable to men, especially to those who love to tell ethnic jokes or dirty humor of some type.

"Now it may happen that a woman sets out to destroy good feelings between neighbors by telling go'odiodia'se (stories that augment by repetition). Now this woman goes to a house and says, "I love you and because I do I will tell you a secret. The woman in the next house speaks evil of you." Now heretofore the two women had been friends but upon hearing this story, the woman becomes an enemy of her former friend. Then the evil story-teller goes to the woman whom she lied about and tells her the hard words that the other woman has spoken. Then is the liar happy having started a feud, and she hastens from house to house to tell of it. Now great troubles arise and soon a fight develops, and one woman causes it all. Therefore the Creator is very sad. Tell your people that such things must stop the moment this message is told.

"Now the Creator has ordained another way. He has ordained that human creatures should be kind one to the other and help each other. When a woman visits another house she must help each work in progress and talk pleasantly. If she relates jokes they must always be upon herself. If she speaks harshly of others, the woman of the house must say, "I remember the desires of our Creator. I cannot hear what you say. I cannot take that evil story." So the trouble is ended there. Now the Creator says that the woman is true who refuses to hear evil reports. She cuts off the evil at its beginning and it does not come from her. So she has won favor before the Creator."

Regarding pride and vanity, they had this to say. "The Creator who made you is sad. The Creator made every person with a different face. Now a man talks saying that he is far more handsome than other men. He boasts that he is exceedingly handsome and grand. But the Creator says all this is very wrong. The vain must repent and never boast again." So they said.

"Now animals seem alike to you. A wild animal that you have once seen you cannot easily say you have seen again. But people are different before you. Now when a man is handsome let him thank his Creator for his comeliness." So they said.

"Now furthermore a man says 'I am the strongest man of all. There is no one who can throw me to the ground.' A man who talks thus is a boaster before the people. Now the Creator says that such boasting is evil. The Creator endowed the man with strength and therefore he should not boast but thank the giver who is the Creator. So tell your people these things." So they said.

"Now furthermore a man says, 'I am the swiftest runner of the world. No one can outrun me.' Now he regards himself as a mighty man and boasts before his people. Now the Creator says that such boasting is evil. The Creator endowed the man with his speed and he should offer thanks and not boast. So we, the messengers, say your people must cease their boasting."

Other messages given to Handsome Lake were to the effect that giving your neighbor a helping hand in some difficult task was a good thing, but that taking things which didn't belong to you was wrong. Also, excessive dancing was viewed with certain disdain by God: "It is not right for you to have so many dances and dance songs;...tell your people that these things must cease; tell them to repent and cease." [Parker noted that "the Seneca had 33 dances...," which in the Creator's view was sinful].

However, God permitted the Seneca to enjoy four "amusements devised in the heaven world, the Osto'wago'wa [the Great Feather dance], Goneowo^n [the Harvest dance], Ado^{n}we^n [the Sacred Song] and Ganawe^n'gowa [the Peach Stone game]. They were to be used during specially ordained periods of thankful worship given to the Almighty for His kind blessings shed forth upon the Iroquois.

"The Creator has sanctioned four dances for producing a joyful spirit and he has placed them in the keeping of Honon'diont [overseers or keepers of ceremonies] who have authority over them. The Creator has ordered that on certain times and occasions there should be thanksgiving ceremonies. At such times, all must thank the Creator that they live. After that, let the chiefs thank him for the ground and the things on the ground and then upward to the sky and the heaven-world where he is. Let the children and old folk come and give thanks. Let the old women who can scarcely walk come. They may lean against the middle benches and after listening to three or four songs must say, I thank the Great Ruler that I have seen this day. Then will the Creator call them right before him."

"It seems that you have never known that when Osto' wago'wa [the Great Feather dance] was being celebrated that one of the four beings was in the midst of it, but it is so. Now when the time for dancing comes you must wash your faces and comb your hair, paint your face with red spots on either cheek, and with a thankful heart go to the ceremony. This preparation will be sufficient, therefore, do not let your style of dress hold you back."

In ancient Israel dancing was considered a proper way to celebrate one's thankfulness to God. Exodus 15:20-21 informs us that, after God saved the Hebrews from Pharoah's armies by drowning them in the Red Sea, Moses' sister, Miriam "took a timbrel in her hand; and all the women went out after her with timbrels and with dances" to express their utmost gratitude unto Him for delivering them from the Egyptians that day. II Samuel 6:14-23 mentions that "David danced before the Lord with all his might...with shouting, and with the sound of the trumpet...leaping and dancing before the Lord." King Saul's daughter, upon seeing him do this, however, "despised him in her heart," but he told her he had been justified in what he did and that God had accepted his dancing as an offering of gratitude unto Him.

These four messengers also informed Handsome Lake that the Devil sends out his invisible emissaries, who follow people around whispering in their ears to do wrong. "Now it is the messenger of the evil spirit that argues thus. Now know you that the evil spirit will hinder you in all good things but you can outwit him by doing the things that he does not wish you to do." Important to note here is the fact that only a humble and contrite spirit is a sure guarantee against the temptations of the Evil One. A proud heart, lofty looks, vain imagination, and an arrogant attitude will always make a person susceptible to the wiles of the Devil.

They told this Seneca prophet to warn his people against the needless and unwanton hunting of animals; they should only kill those they needed for meat or clothing, and no more than this. "At some future day, the wild animals will become extinct," they warned him, so the careful preservation of the remaining game in those days was absolutely essential to their well-being. How prophetic their words have turned out to be!

Handsome Lake learned from them that "there are [different] grades of sin." Parker noted in his footnote that "the higher the position [in life] the greater the sin." They explained to the Seneca prophet that while most men and women would have desires to repent of their sins, yet the Evil One would induce them every way possible not to. Yet "the Creator will not give up hope of them until they pass from the earth; it is only then that they can lose their souls if they have not repented; so the Creator always hopes for repentance."

These heavenly messengers also gave him a better understanding of Hell than what *Bible*-believing Christians seem to have. They told Handsome Lake that bad and unrepentant souls still remained upon this earth, only mortals couldn't see them, just feel their evil presence. Such souls might continue lingering around their places of former habitation or employment. They also preferred garbage dumps, abandoned wagons and buggies [in modern times this would be junked cars and trucks], swamps and marshes, dark caves, and any other place unsuitable or disliked by mortals. This concept differs radically from the old Catholic and Protestant notions of a literal burning inferno type of Hell complete with lakes of fire and brimstone, flowing rivers of lava, naked people shoveling coal, and horned and cloven-footed devils with pitchforks prodding them on.

Handsome Lake learned too that there can be different levels of wicked spirits. Some of the worst were those who had once been bad shamans or medicine-men; in modern lingo, real religious devils who may once have been ministers or priests of various denominations. Lower on the scale were brutish devils without much class or tact to them; these would have been former warriors or common squaws of rather base morals. Somewhere in between would be mischievous imps or those who lied, cheated, and stole in mortality. There were also a goodly number of wicked spirits given over to addictions like gambling, rum or whiskey drinking, sexual promiscuity, and so forth. They still possessed their former addictions of the flesh in the spirit, but without the flesh, they could no longer satisfy these awful lusts and desires, although these still continued in their souls. Now all of these various classes of wicked spirits were organized into tribes and groups with chiefs and sub-chiefs over them, with the Evil One himself at the top of all. And it was their main task to destroy or mislead humans still living on earth in the flesh.

·"Now another message to tell your people," they continued. "Chiefs and high officers have spoken derisively of each other and quarreled. What they have done must not be done again." Parker's footnote explains that the "green-eyed monster" of "jealousy was the principle cause of the dissension that led to the decay of the League of the Iroquois."

One of the most significant teachings they gave to him was an understanding of a pre-mortal life, a mortal life, and a post-mortal life, which Handsome Lake summarized this way: "Then the messengers told me that my life journey would be in three stages, and when I entered the third I would enter into the eternity of the New World, the land of our Creator, so they said." This differs radically from the presumed Christian notions and the erroneous Hindu belief in reincarnation, but compares favorably with the Mormon belief in "eternal progression."

Handsome Lake's visitors also introduced him to the idea that God and Lucifer occasionally meet somewhere on neutral ground to debate the condition of the children of men on earth. There is a striking similarity between what they shared with him and what is contained in the *Bible* in the First and Second Chapters of Job. In both instances, we find a dialogue ensuing between the forces of light and truth and those of darkness and despair.

"There is a dispute in the heaven-world between two parties. It is a controversy about you, the children of earth. Two great beings are disputing—one is the Great Ruler, the Creator, and the other is the evil-minded spirit. You who are on earth do not know the things of heaven.

"Now the evil one said, 'I am the ruler of the earth because when I command I speak but once and man obeys.'

"Then answered the Great Ruler, 'The earth is mine for I have created it and you have helped me in no part.'

"Now the evil one answered, 'I do not acknowledge that you have created the earth and that I helped in no part, but I say that when I say to men, Obey me, they straightway obey, but they do not hear your voice.'

"Then the Great Ruler replied, 'Truly the children are my own for they have never done evil.'

"And the evil one answering said, 'Nay, the children are mine for when I bid one saying, Pick up that stick and strike your fellow, they obey me quickly. Aye, the children are mine.'

"Then was the Great Ruler very sad and he said, 'Once more will I send my messengers and tell them my heart and they will tell my people and thus I will redeem my own.'

"Then the evil one replied, 'Even so it will not be long before men transgress your commands. I can destroy it with a word for they will do my bidding.'

"Now at that time the Great Ruler spoke to the four messengers saying, 'Go tell mankind that...the evil one...is he who will punish the wicked when they depart from this world.'"

Compare all of this with Job 1:6-12; 2:1-7. Here are found some similarities, especially in the fact that God and Lucifer apparently meet together on neutral ground from time to time to discuss the affairs of people on earth.

"Now there was a day when the sons of God came to present themselves before the Lord, and Satan came also among them. And the Lord said unto Satan, Whence comest thou? Then Satan answered the Lord, and said, From going to and fro in the earth, and from walking up and down in it.

"And the Lord said unto Satan, Hast thou considered my servant Job, that there is none like him in the earth, a perfect and an upright man, one that feareth God, and escheweth evil?

"Then Satan answered the Lord, and said, Doth Job fear God for nought? Hast not thou made an hedge about him and about his house, and about all that he hath on every side? Thou hast blessed the work of his hands, and his substance is increased in the land. But put forth thine hand now, and touch all that he hath, and he will curse thee to thy face.

"And the Lord said unto Satan, Behold, all that he hath is in thy power; only upon himself put not forth thine hand. So Satan went forth from the presence of the Lord."

This same occasional getting together occurred at another time as Chapter 2 reveals: "Again there was a day when the sons of God came to present themselves before the Lord, and Satan came also among them to present himself before the Lord." Then a repetition of nearly the same dialogue follows between both parties concerning the affairs of Job.

Both examples—the message to Handsome Lake and the Holy *Bible* incident—demonstrate the fact that the affairs of men and women on earth are frequently discussed not only in the heavens, but also on neutral ground somewhere between God and Lucifer. God will introduce a topic and Satan will respond in kind to it or else just give a report of what he is currently doing on the earth. Satan will always ask for more than he gets, but has to be satisfied with what is granted unto him in the way of hurting or harming the children of men. From both accounts we learn that limitations are always placed on what he can and cannot do.

Later sections in "The Great Message" of the Four Messengers dealt with "judging diseases and prescribing remedies." Here we learn that while God has ordained certain plants for the healing of the sick, so likewise, does Satan have his own counterparts in the form of harmful plants which can induce illness or even bring about death.

The four messengers who visited Handsome Lake on various occasions, instructed him in the ceremony that was always to be used when gathering wild plants for medical purposes. "Now let this be your ceremony when you wish to employ the medicine in a plant: First offer tobacco. Then tell the plant in gentle words what you desire of it and pluck it from the roots. It is said in the upper world that it is not right to take a plant for medicine without first talking to it. Let not one ever be taken without first speaking."

Arthur C. Parker's commentary on this was as follows: "When a Seneca wishes to gather medicinal herbs, he goes into the woods where they grow and builds a small fire. When there is a quantity of glowing embers, he stands before it and as he speaks, at intervals he casts a pinch of tobacco on the coals. He speaks to the spirits of the medicines telling them that he desires their healing virtues to cure his people of their afflictions.

"You have said that you are ready to heal the earth," chants the gatherer of herbs, "so now I claim you for my medicine. Give me of your healing virtues to purge and cleanse and cure. I will not destroy you but plant your seed that you may come again and yield fourfold more. Spirits of the herbs, I do not take your lives without purposes but to make you the agent of healing for we are very sick. You have said that all the world might come to you, so I have come. I give you thanks for your benefits and thank the Creator for your gift."

When the last puff of tobacco smoke had arisen the gatherer of herbs begins his work. He digs the plants from the roots and breaking off the seed stalks drops the pods into the hole and gently covers them over with fertile leaf mold. "The plant will come again," he says "and I have not destroyed life but helped increase it. So the plant is willing to lend me of its virtue."

"Now another message," they continued with Handsome Lake. "It has been a custom when a person knows of a healing herb to ask payment for giving it to a patient. Now we say that this is not right. It is not right to demand compensation for treating the sick. If such is done it adds greater afflictions to the sick one. The Creator has given different people knowledge of different things and it is the Creator's desire that men should employ their knowledge to help one another, especially those who are afflicted. Now moreover the person helped out ought only to give tobacco for an offering." So they said and he said. Eniaiehuk.

Upon one occasion, the four messengers took the spirit of Handsome Lake with them into Heaven, while his body remained in a comatose state inside his cabin or lodge. (The spirit of man or woman is identical to his or her physical body, right down to the last wrinkle, pubic hair, wart, and mole).

"Then they proceeded on their journey but had not gone far when they stopped. Then the messengers said, 'Watch,' and pointed to a certain spot toward the setting sun. So he watched and saw a large object revolving. It was white and moving slowly. Then said the four messengers, 'What did you see?' He answered, 'I saw a large object revolving. It was white and moving slowly.'

"Then said the messengers, it is true. The thing is that which relates the air over the earth. It is that which we call the Oda'eo (the veil over all). It is said that it would bring great calamity should it revolve too fast. Should it turn faster it would injure mankind. Now we are the regulators and watchers of the veil over all.

"They proceeded on their journey and they seemed to be advancing toward an approaching man. Soon they met him and passed. Now when they were a distance apart they turned and he was facing them. They greeted each other. Then said the man, 'Sedwago'wane [Handsome Lake], I must ask you a question. Did you never hear your grandfathers say that once there was a certain man upon the earth across the great waters who was slain by his own people?' That was what he said when he spoke.

"Then answered Sedwago'wane, 'It is true. I have heard my grandparents say this.' Then answered the man, 'I am he.' (Sega^n hedus, He who resurrects). And he turned his palms upward and they were scarred and his feet were likewise and his breast was pierced by a spear wound. It appeared that his hands and feet were torn by iron nails. All this was true. It could be seen and blood was fresh upon him.

"Then said the man, 'They slew me because of their independence and unbelief. So I have gone home to shut the doors of heaven that they may not see me again until the earth passes away. Then will all the people cry to me for succor, and when I come it will be in this wise: my face will be sober and I shall turn it to my people. Now let me ask how your people receive your teachings.'

"He [Handsome Lake] answered, 'It is my opinion that half my people are inclined to believe in me.' Then answered he, 'You are more successful than I for some believe in you but none in me. I am inclined to believe that in the end it will also be so with you... Now tell your people that they will become lost when they follow the ways of the white man.'"

During his heavenly sojourn with these four divine messengers, Handsome Lake learned that stingy and selfish and gluttonous people can never "stand upon the heaven road." Parker's commentary reads thusly: "Those who gain great riches and lack humility cannot stand upon the sky-road nor can they walk on it. The poor and meek only can travel skyward and not even the poor unless their ways have been humble and marked with [considerable] virtue. Thus it is said, 'It is better to be poor on earth and rich in the sky-world than to have earth riches and no heaven.'

"Now they said, 'We shall proceed on.' Now the farther they went the more brilliant the light became. They had not gone far when the four messengers said, 'Now we will stop again. Look attentively at what you see.'

"So he looked and saw three groups of people and each group was of a different size. The first was large, the second small, and the third still smaller. Then the messengers asked him, 'What do you see?' He answered, 'I saw three groups, the first a large group, the second half as large as the first, and the third still smaller.' That is what he said when he answered.

"Then they replied, Truly you have seen. The groups represent the people of earth. The first group you saw was composed of those who have not repented; the second group was inclined half way, and the third group, the smallest one, was composed of those who have repented. They are protected by the true belief in Gai'wiio' [The Great Message of Handsome Lake]."

Handsome Lake died August 10, 1815 on the Seneca Indian reservation in Onondaga County, New York. But to the numbers gathered about him to hear his [final] message [before he died], he said, "I will soon to my new home. Soon I will step into the new world for there is a plain pathway before me leading there. Whoever follows my teachings will follow in my footsteps and I will look back upon him with outstretched arms inviting him into the new world of our Creator. Alas, I fear that a pall of smoke will obscure the eyes of many from the truth of Gai'wiio' but I pray that when I am gone that all may do what I have taught."

Every so often in the history of the human race, there comes an individual out of virtual obscurity who has an undeniable impact on mankind. Such an individual was the Seneca prophet, Handsome Lake. Born into poverty and near death's door at one point, he overcame both handicaps to develop into one of the greatest Indian spiritual leaders that any Native American tribe has ever produced. His four heavenly messengers imparted to him a great deal of wisdom and advice, which eventually revolutionized the very heart of the Seneca culture. His teachings dramatically changed tribal lifestyle forever.

Looking back at what has been presented in this book, a few timely issues stand out. One of these has to do with our earliest ancestors, going back tens of thousands of years. Though not always well coiffed, fashionably attired, or dignified looking, these cave people enjoyed certain things we do not, namely remarkable health and incredible strength. Men could have lifted the front ends of most cars completely off the ground without thinking anything of it. People then ran greater risks of being savagely clawed or trampled to death by angry saber-tooths or mastodons, than of dying from cancer, diabetes, heart disease, or hypertension.

Civilization had to find ways to cleanse the inner man and woman of all the toxins produced by eating over-cooked and refined foods. What the Egyptians came up with were the historic enema and herbal purges. While often dramatic in their administered results, they accomplished the task of purifying the body and blood. The Babylonians expanded these ancient cleansing rituals to include the liver, which they believed was the seat of life, or place where the soul of man and woman resided. Keeping this organ in tip-top shape insured that the rest of the body would enjoy near perfect health, too.

The Babylonians also believed strongly in the principle of divining. They resorted to reading the livers of countless sacrificed sheep and working with rods or arrows in order to understand the mind and will of their gods pertaining to everyday affairs. The Hebrews also employed interesting methods of divination as well— the most common being the casting of lots. Detailed information on how this can be safely done can be found in a previous chapter. Even looking to the stars for answers isn't always a bad idea, though this author doesn't subscribe to everything claimed be modern astrology.

The Children of Israel subsisted on manna in the wilderness for 40 years. The true identity of this mysterious, divinely provided staple has pretty much remained a mystery for most scholars. But recent scientific reexamination of the whole matter, suggests the likelihood of it having been a form of chlorella, a freshwater alga packed with nutritional vitality. Moses gave the Children of Israel some nutritional guidelines, which if followed in our own time, would guarantee that we would be sick less often than we are now. Among these guidelines would be refraining from pork, chicken, and all shellfish.

The ancient Israelites also loved garlic. We find recorded in Numbers 11:5 a fond remembrance for this spice in these poignant words: "We remember the fish, which we did eat in Egypt freely... and the garlic." Herodotus, the Greek historian, writing of these former pyramid builders, reported: "There is an inscription in Egyptian characters on the pyramid which records the quantity of radishes, onions, and garlic consumed by the laborers who constructed it; and I remember perfectly well that the interpreter who read the writing to me said that the money thus expended was 1600 talents of silver." In modern currency, this amounts to about $4,000,000 U.S. The Japanese in modern times have perfected garlic by a remarkably slow aging process that, from start to finish, usually takes four years. This kyolic garlic has become the world's superior garlic in terms of nutritional vitality and medical strength.

From China have come unusual but effective methods of diagnosing and treating illnesses of different descriptions. The many methods of diagnoses fall into four basic categories: visual inspection, hearing and smelling, questioning the patient directly, and physically touching the person's body. By these means a determination can be made of what is wrong with the patient. Some aspects of the physical examination involving the hands and feet also double as treatments too; in this case, reflexology or acupressure. One of the most accurate methods of detection is to take one's own pulse, which requires a little experience before becoming reasonably proficient at it. But the extra time spent in properly learning it is well worth the effort. Some of the simplest detections can be made by observing body sounds or carefully inspecting bodily discharges like the feces or urine. Other methods, such as looking at the tongue, can give an entire history of the liver.

Chinese herbal medicine has contributed much to the healing arts, as well. For many centuries the Chinese knowledge of herbs has proven to be quite superior to that of other civilizations. For instance, there is no comparison between the herbal medicine of medieval Europe steeped in all its superstitious nonsense with the more empirical and medically advanced Chinese herbal system. Individual herbs, as well as formulas such as those provided by Li Chung Yun, have made Chinese herbal medicine very effective and invited the scientific community to investigate it more closely in recent years.

But as everyone involved in holistic health or medical wellness ought to know by now, you just cannot have good health for the body without doing something for the soul as well. To this end, then, were the last two chapters of this book devoted for the purpose of spiritually nourishing our inner souls. The information presented has been largely drawn from many Native American tribes which once resided in large numbers in both North and South America. These peoples, more than any others, seem to have grasped the very essence of what true religion is all about. Their simple beliefs are free from the usual nonsense of reincarnation and similar things to have come out of the east.

It is to this end and for these several different reasons that this book was written in the hopes that all who are fortunate enough to be guided to the messages within its pages may find comfort and strength in what they read. May the physical and spiritual treasures embodied herein remain with you always in your mortal and resurrected journeys through infinity.

APPENDIX

Further information on Neanderthal diets and ancient folk remedies may be obtained by writing the author in care of the organization and address given below. To obtain free copies of two books on garlic, send ten 30 cent stamps to the address below.

Dr. John Heinerman, Director
Anthropological Research Center
P.O. Box 11471
Salt Lake City, UT 84147
(801)521-8824

To obtain information on Chinese medicine and supplies of top quality Chinese herbs and the Li Chung Yun herbal formulas, contact:

Canada
Albi Imports Limited
7188 Curragh Ave.
Burnaby, B.C. V5J 4V9
(800)663-0628
(604)438-2029

U.S.A.
Albi Imports Limited
19029 36th Ave. West
Unit B, Bldg. C Colony Park
Lynnwood, WA. 98036
(206)778-9494

To obtain the published proceedings of the First World Garlic Congress, write for price inquiry to:

Nutrition International
6 Silverfern Drive,
Irvine, CA 92715

Nutritional Intl.
POB 6043
Irvine, CA 92716-6043
(714)854-8095

To obtain plain liquid kyolic garlic, liquid kyolic with vitamins B_1 and B_{12}, powdered kyolic garlic with brewer's yeast and kelp, powdered kyolic garlic with selenium and vitamins A and E, powdered kyolic garlic with vitamin C and astragalus, kyolic garlic with vitamin E, cayenne, and hawthorn berry, powdered kyolic garlic with lecithin, powdered kyolic garlic with special enzymes, powdered kyolic garlic hi-po (high potency), kyo-green, kyo-dophilus, and ginkoolic, call or write:

Wakunaga of America Co. Ltd.
23501 Madero
Mission Viejo, CA 92691
(800)421-2998 (in CA) (800)544-5800

To obtain my previous two New Age books, *Spiritual Wisdom of The Native Americans and People in Space*, send $19.90 plus $4.00 shipping/handling to:

Cassandra Press
P.O. Box 868
San Rafael, CA 94915
(415)382-8507

INDEX